Contents

Preface   vii

1   Introduction   1

2   Literature Review   17

3   How the Research was Conducted   39

4   What Keyworkers Do   52

5   How Keyworkers Leave   78

6   Feelings After Leaving: Clients' Stories   108

7   Feelings After Leaving: Staff's Stories   125

8   Why is it Hard to Say Goodbye?   145

9   Saying Goodbye: Recommendations for
    Services   161

Appendix A: Interview Schedule for Residents   181

Appendix B: Interview Schedule for Staff   185

Appendix C: Interview with 'Eve'   188

Appendix D: Interview with 'Gill'   202

References   218

Index   226

Ev'ry time we say goodbye I die a little.
Ev'ry time we say goodbye I wonder why a little.
Why the gods above me, who must be in the know,
Think so little of me they allow you to go.

Saying Goodbye

When keyworker relationships end

Victoria Mattison and Nancy Pistrang

FREE ASSOCIATION BOOKS / LONDON / NEW YORK

First published in Great Britain 2000 by
Free Association Books
57 Warren Street
London W1T 5NR

Copyright © Victoria Mattison and Nancy Pistrang 2000

ISBN 1 85343 510 4 pbk

09 08 07 06 05 04 03 02 01 00
10 9   8   7   6   5   4   3   2   1

A CIP record for this book is available from the British Library

Designed, typeset and produced for
Free Association Books Ltd by
Chase Publishing Services
Printed in the European Union by Athenaeum Press,
Gateshead, England

Preface

This book was inspired by personal experiences of working with people with learning disabilities and their carers. One of us (Victoria Mattison), having worked for some years in the field, was struck by the frequency of referrals to clinical psychology services which coincided with the departure of clients' keyworkers. It seemed obvious that the timing of these referrals was significant. The keyworker's departure often left a client distressed – although this distress was often unacknowledged by staff and frequently expressed indirectly by the client, for example, in the form of difficult behaviour.

People with learning disabilities living in residential care regularly experience separation and loss when their keyworkers move away. Frequent staff turnover, which often results from organisational difficulties in retaining staff, can have devastating effects on the lives of clients. Our clinical experience suggests that these transitions are critical for the emotional well-being of clients, to whom supportive relationships with staff are essential. Many of these clients have spent a lifetime in institutional care, and the majority will never become fully independent in daily living.

Our main aim in writing this book is to raise awareness of what happens when keyworker relationships end. We hope the book will offer staff and clinicians an understanding of the feelings both clients and staff may have when separations occur. We also hope to highlight some wider issues about the friendships and relationships that adults with learning disabilities have (or don't have), and the role of keyworkers in filling a void in the lives of people who are often socially isolated. We make some specific recommendations for how services can plan for the end of staff–client relationships, with the aim of making such endings less painful and disruptive for clients and staff alike.

The book grew out of a doctoral research study carried out by Victoria Mattison and supervised by Nancy Pistrang. (The term 'we' is used throughout the book, but the interviews were conducted by Victoria Mattison alone, and the clinical experiences referred to are also drawn from her own work.) The original study involved in-depth interviews with both clients and staff in residential settings for people with learning disabilities. We draw extensively on the words of participants themselves, presenting clients' and staff members' parallel accounts of loss and change. The heart of the book tells the stories of clients and staff: how their relationships ended and the feelings that they had at the time. We have changed the names of all clients and staff in order to protect their confidentiality.

People with learning disabilities are rarely asked about their experiences of care. We hope that, in telling their stories in this book, we will allow their voices to be heard. This book can only begin to raise awareness of how important the process of saying goodbye is to the welfare of clients. However, we hope that the clients' and staff's accounts presented in the book will enable our readers to think differently about – and perhaps make more sense of – the process of saying goodbye.

The book is principally aimed at carers of adults with learning disabilities. It is intended as a resource for staff working with clients in the community, families of people with learning disabilities, multidisciplinary practitioners, voluntary and social services and NHS psychology services. It is also intended for students and professionals in psychology, social work, nursing and related fields.

We would like to express our gratitude to the adults with learning disabilities and the keyworkers who took part in our study: without their openness and willingness to talk about their experiences, the study would have been impossible. We are enormously grateful to Chris Roberts for helping to get the study off the ground and for providing continued support and encouragement throughout the duration of the project.

Thanks also to the multidisciplinary teams at Harrow, Tower Hamlets and Camden and Islington Learning Disabilities Services, as well as the North East Thames Learning Disabilities Special Interest Group, who thoughtfully discussed the research findings and shared ideas about recommendations for services. Several people helped us to clarify our thinking, ploughed through various drafts of the book and made invaluable comments: in particular, we want to thank Chris Barker, Linda Clare, Sheila Mattison, Helen Quigley, Katrina Scior, Sarah Walden and Suzanne Wilson. Free Association Books made the process of publication as stress-free as possible: thanks to David Stonestreet for his continual enthusiasm and useful suggestions, and to Ray Addicott at Chase Publishing Services for seeing the typescript through to a finished book. We are also grateful to Warner Chappell Music Limited for allowing us to quote a few lines from Cole Porter's song 'Ev'ry Time We Say Goodbye'.

Finally, we would like to thank Claudio, Chris, Jessie and Anna for allowing this book to become part of their lives (and disrupt their evenings and weekends) over the past year and for their endless support and encouragement.

CHAPTER 1

Introduction

Kevin was a client whose keyworker had left a few months previously. As part of our research, we interviewed both Pete, Kevin's keyworker, and Debbie, a staff member who observed Kevin's reaction after Pete left. The two staff members talked about how they thought Kevin felt about the separation.

Pete tended to play down Kevin's reaction. He said:

> *I knew that Kevin wouldn't be affected emotionally. I knew that it might stress him out a bit, but as for kind of feeling a loss, he wouldn't really feel a loss. I really felt that he would only really miss the fact that there was something there for two years, and now it was gone ... It was kind of a comfort thing, there was something missing, and that was me – I could have been an object. I knew that he didn't really understand emotion.*

However, in contrast, Debbie recalled Kevin's becoming very upset:

> *Kevin became really quiet. It became really noticeable that he was really unhappy. He completely withdrew from what was going on. It was unbelievable. He was unhappy all the time. He wouldn't eat at the dinner table. He would throw his plate on the floor. We couldn't believe it.*

As this brief illustration shows, clients can be deeply affected by the loss of a staff member who has worked closely with them. However, keyworkers may not appreciate the importance of their relationship and the distress that may be caused by their departure, and different staff members may have very different views of the same event. In this case, Pete was either unaware of, or unable to acknowledge, the effect of his departure on his client. For Debbie, who was around to observe Kevin following Pete's departure, there was a realisation that whilst the client did not respond verbally to his loss, he seemed to manifest his feelings through his behaviours.

Our own experiences of working in services for adults with learning disabilities have made us aware of the emotional upheaval that can occur when keyworkers in residential (and daycare) settings move away. Of course, not all keyworkers are missed: some clients undoubtedly feel a sense of relief when a keyworker with whom they have not got on well leaves. But, for many clients living in residential settings, the keyworker is one of the most important figures in their life, and the relationship between them may be one of the closest clients experience. How the keyworker's departure is handled – for example, how the client is told – can have a critical impact not only on the client, but on other residents in the home, the staff, and the new keyworker who is faced with supporting someone who has experienced a significant loss.

Sadly, many people with learning disabilities have limited opportunities for making lasting friendships and relationships. For the significant numbers who do not live with their families and who have often grown up in institutional care systems, relationships with staff can be central. However, the changes in staff that occur regularly in care settings may serve to exacerbate the dependency on others and the lack of control that adults with learning disabilities have over important aspects of their lives.

In this first chapter, we aim to 'set the scene' for our study of the endings of staff–client relationships. We consider wider issues relating to care in the community, the emotional lives of clients, and the political and social context of care for people with learning disabilities. We also present a case example from our own clinical experience which highlights some of the issues germane to the ending of staff–client relationships.

Care in the Community

A recent national strategic survey has indicated that one third of all adults with learning disabilities live in staffed homes (Wallace, 2000). We know that within these settings, residents' relationships with staff are important – particularly in the absence of friendships and other social roles. A high turnover of staff is also a typical feature of many of these residential settings. So what happens when staff leave? If services are to address the emotional needs and experiences of adults with learning disabilities, then we must think carefully about the repeated experiences of separation which clients often endure.

Services and support for people with learning disabilities have changed considerably in recent years. The last two decades have seen a process of resettlement of adults with learning disabilities from large institutions into the community, driven by the ideas of normalisation and by government policy (Bailey and Cooper, 1999). The philosophy of normalisation (Wolfensberger, 1972, 1983) was intended to enable people with learning disabilities to live as normal a life as possible – for example, to be able to participate in community activities and to make relationships with non-learning-disabled adults. Wolfensberger's ideas about social acceptability, integration, choice and participation (which underpin the philosophy of normalisation) played a major role in guiding service planning and development. An important consequence of de-institutionalisation has been the provision of smaller 'family-like' homes in the community.

However, in many ways there has been a failure to achieve what normalisation set out to do. Despite the community locations of their new homes, residents often are not integrated into the community and have limited choices about how to conduct their lives. Many people in community homes are more isolated than they have ever been. While de-institutionalisation was partly based on a progressive philosophy (and partly based on a desire to cut costs), its implementation has not always been successful (Brechin and Swain, 1989). In practice, clients' interests have often been overlooked.

Perhaps one of the most disturbing findings from studies following the process of de-institutionalisation comes from the work of Landesman-Dwyer and Berkson (1984), who found that those clients with more severe and profound disabilities were the most vulnerable after moving into the community. Although these clients had previously shown the most difficulty with initiating contacts with others, many nonetheless had clear ties to other clients. When these ties were broken after leaving the long-stay institutions, levels of social interaction were considerably reduced. Not only did these clients not find new and lasting relationships with others, but they were also at risk of being overlooked and ignored by new people in their environment. Clients of all levels of ability were often separated from those they liked and, in some cases, they were placed in homes with clients who they would have preferred to avoid.

Many adults with learning disabilities – especially those who came through the large long-stay institutions as children – have high levels of social problems. The adversity they have experienced often makes it difficult for them to relate to others. However, the smaller community homes that have replaced the large institutions of the past do not seem to have facilitated the development of relationships and friendships between clients. Smaller homes often seem to heighten the importance of the relationship between staff and clients, rather than that between clients. In the old long-stay institutions, clients were often free to move about the usually large grounds and seek out a range of individuals for social contact, whilst in community homes clients are mostly dependent on staff to leave their own front doors. The role of staff in community homes is all-encompassing: it includes not only planning and facilitating the clients' care and support, but living with clients and being part of their daily lives. It is not surprising, therefore, that these relationships can become very close. As a result, staff may experience discomfort when clients appear to become 'over-dependent' on them – especially when clients' life experiences have led to their having very strong dependency needs (Firth and Rapley, 1990). Our impression is that staff are given little preparation or support to help them deal with these issues that inevitably arise as part of the demanding task of providing intimate care for others.

The Emotional Lives of People with Learning Disabilities

Services for people with learning disabilities have often neglected the emotional lives and experiences of the people in their care (Arthur, 1999). A history of behavioural modification and an emphasis on cognitive development have been dominant in the field of psychology and learning disabilities. Although behavioural approaches do pay attention to psychological factors affecting people's behaviour, they focus primarily on behaviours rather than emotions. As Arthur (1999) points out, the emotional development and inner worlds of adults with learning disabilities are rarely described in the clinical or research literature. Although much attention has been paid to the philosophy of normalisation, normalisation itself can be criticised for its lack of interest in the subjective experiences of adults with learning disabilities (Bender, 1993).

Ideas arising from psychodynamic and humanistic schools of psychology have influenced the thinking behind this book. Both of these traditions place a central importance on people's feelings in relation to one another. Over the last two decades, there has been a growing interest in applying psychodynamic ideas to the field of learning disabilities. In an influential paper entitled 'The psychopathology of handicap', Bicknell (1983) described the emotional problems faced by people with learning disabilities and the importance of understanding what it means, for clients themselves, to be 'handicapped'. In particular, Bicknell pointed to the 'bereavement' responses of parents to having a handicapped child and the subsequent problems which the handicapped person and the family face at different stages of the life-cycle.

There is now a small body of evidence suggesting that people with learning disabilities can benefit from individual psychotherapy (see Beail, 1995, 1998). Several case studies (for example, Symington, 1981; Beail, 1989; Sinason, 1992) provide anecdotal evidence for the positive changes that can occur when clients are given the opportunity to explore and express their feelings. A few studies (for example, Frankish, 1989; Beail, 1998) provide more systematic outcome data, indicating that psychotherapy can reduce behavioural problems and improve clients' general level of functioning.

Sinason (1986) also points out how trauma, particularly in relation to loss, can exacerbate handicap. She suggests that many people with learning disabilities develop 'secondary handicap' – that is, characteristics or ways of behaving that make them appear more disabled – as a defence against the impact of trauma. In this way, when trauma is not acknowledged, people become increasingly disabled: their underlying organic handicap becomes exaggerated. Sinason's work points to the importance of thinking about clients' repeated experiences of separation and loss in relation to their development. Offering clients opportunities for processing their feelings seems crucial if they are to reach their full potential.

People working with adults with learning disabilities frequently underestimate their clients' emotional capacity. This is particularly true for clients who are more severely disabled: even these clients can be responsive when they are given the space to process their feelings (Sinason, 1992). It can be difficult for care staff and clinicians to think about the meaning behind their clients' behaviours. As other writers have pointed out (for example, Bailey et al., 1986), we do not know much about the feelings of adults with learning disabilities or how their feelings are communicated to others. Perhaps we prefer not to know: in many ways it is easier to simply attend to the more practical and physical aspects of their care. Yet how can we ignore such critical aspects of people's lives as their emotional experiences? Agencies that provide a caring service must be able to address the emotional needs of their clients. We therefore need to ask such questions as: how are people with learning disabilities affected by their experiences of loss, grief, change, happiness, or new relationships?

Our own work as clinical psychologists has impressed upon us the potential for emotional turmoil caused by staff departures. In our experience, many referrals to specialist learning disability services come in the wake of a sudden and unprepared-for loss of a keyworker. Frequently the request is for 'behavioural management' of a client who exhibits disturbed behaviour. The referral often makes little mention of the client's emotional experience of loss, emphasising instead the more concrete behavioural problems. However, our individual therapeutic work with clients has strikingly revealed the emotions behind the behaviours: feelings of loss and abandonment, and a reluctance to become attached to new staff for fear of being abandoned without warning again. We present a brief case example, below, as an illustration.

A Case Example

While we were writing this book, one of us (VM) was working with a client called Ruby (not her real name). Ruby was a 56-year-old woman with learning disabilities and long-standing mental health problems. She had spent a lifetime in institutional care, with multiple changes of keyworkers, and she now shared her home with two other clients in a staffed house in the community. Ruby's parents had placed her in care at a very young age, after struggling to cope with her at home. She retained some contact with her family, including one sister, who lived a few hours away, and her niece. However, her niece had recently left the country unexpectedly, due to a job opportunity that had suddenly arisen.

Ruby's referral to the specialist learning disability team coincided with a staff member leaving the home after four years. The team's psychiatrist reported a deterioration in Ruby's emotional state and a return of behavioural patterns which had concerned the staff and other clients in the home. It was agreed with Ruby and the staff at her home that she would come for weekly counselling sessions and that we would review our work after one year. About nine months after the counselling started, Ruby's keyworker, Helen, left her home unexpectedly and without warning. Ruby gave us permission to tell the following story about Helen's departure. It is told from the psychologist's point of view.

Helen was Ruby's keyworker and confidante and they had enjoyed a close and constant keyworking relationship for seven years. Helen was a sensitive and thoughtful young woman who seemed warm and respectful towards Ruby. She accompanied Ruby to most of our counselling sessions, supporting her during her journey and sitting in the waiting room until we finished our sessions. Ruby would often leave the session for a couple of minutes in the middle to check that Helen was still there waiting for her. She would then return to the room, reassured.

On the day of one of the sessions, Helen telephoned to tell me that she was leaving her job and saying goodbye to Ruby the following day. She had not yet told Ruby. She explained that she had felt very unsupported by the manager and the other staff at the home and that she had found the work overwhelming in recent months. Helen agreed to tell Ruby about her departure before our session that afternoon. Later that day, the two women arrived together for the session as usual and, as we left the waiting room, Helen mouthed to me, 'She took it very well.'

At the start of our session Ruby sat for a moment and began to talk about what she had been doing at the day centre. After a short time I said I wondered how she was and what she understood about what was happening at the home. Ruby stood up and left the room abruptly. I followed her to the waiting room and suggested that perhaps we could talk together with Helen about what was happening. Ruby seemed pleased with that suggestion and promptly led Helen into the room. I suggested that we might use the time we had together as an opportunity for the two women to say goodbye and to think about the work they had done together and the memories they had of their relationship. It felt difficult to know where to begin, until Helen started to talk about the lovely holidays they had shared, the places they had visited and the activities they had enjoyed at home. We thought for a moment about what Ruby might remember about Helen. After a brief silence, Ruby looked up at Helen and said simply, 'That I liked her.' Helen began to cry and Ruby seemed shocked and became quiet. She then said pleadingly, 'Don't cry, Helen.' Helen explained that she was crying because she felt sad to leave Ruby and to say goodbye after such a long time.

Ruby and Helen then began to reminisce together about their past experiences of spending time together, and about the people in Ruby's family who Helen had met. She explained that she wanted to see Ruby in the future, to invite her to her home and spend time together again. After another few minutes Ruby said that she had had enough of talking and that she wanted to go home. The painful feelings were difficult to tolerate for all of us.

Later that day Helen telephoned from the home. She explained that she had known that it was not right to leave Ruby so suddenly and without warning, but that the circumstances in the home had forced her to leave. She had been worried and afraid about telling Ruby. She was very sad and seemed overwhelmed by her feelings of guilt.

The following week Ruby came to her session as usual. She said straight away, 'I feel sad today, because it would be Mum's anniversary.' She had not spoken to Helen during the week. It seemed that her keyworker's departure from the home had put her in touch with her feelings of loss and grief. After a few moments she asked with urgency, 'When are you leaving?' Her confidence had been shaken and everyone seemed transient to her. I became very aware of the relative brevity of our own contact and the fact that we too had a planned ending in the next few months.

Soon after Helen left, Ruby was allocated a new keyworker in the home, who telephoned me to check when our sessions were planned for the following weeks. During our conversation, I said that I wondered how things had been since Helen left. The new keyworker explained that, due to all the paperwork and plans for transfer of care, she had not had much time to spend with Ruby, so it was difficult to know.

This case illustrates some of the difficulties staff and clients may experience in saying goodbye. It also illustrates that beginnings and endings are an integral part of the life-cycle of staff and clients in residential care settings. There are many keyworkers who are clearly good at their jobs throughout the time they work in a home. They may be conscientious and sensitive in all aspects of what they do, but they will often avoid the final task of saying goodbye. This avoidance may arise from their lack of awareness of their own importance to clients, or as Helen's response illustrates, their understanding that saying goodbye is critically important to the emotional world of the client, but emotionally quite daunting to initiate. Perhaps the staff are often left feeling uncertain about what to do and how to face some of the pain of separation.

The Political and Social Context

Any discussion of the relationships between people with learning disabilities and care staff must take note of the wider political and social issues which are inherent to the context of residential care. Providing good-quality care is not just about policies, procedures or implementing recommendations; it is also about the importance and respect given to people with learning disabilities as a client group and learning disability carers as a staff group. These two are intrinsically linked.

Caring is a function which does not hold high status. Care staff in residential units are often poorly paid; work long, hard hours; and receive little training, support or supervision. The majority of the staff are women, and many are from minority ethnic communities: they come from sections of society which are the least empowered. These staff are expected to implement complicated and demanding arrangements for the management, support and care of clients with complex needs. The poor conditions of work often lead to burnout, withdrawal and high rates of staff turnover. One could argue that care staff frequently are devalued, like the clients with whom they work: they are attributed little respect and are not viewed as worthy of training. Such poor conditions of work, and other people's attitudes, can affect the self-esteem of the carers themselves, who may internalise a devalued view of their role.

We have alluded earlier to the failure of many community homes to facilitate friendships between residents, which may result in the 'over-dependence' of residents on staff. This issue can be viewed within a wider political perspective, taking into account the social status and histories of adults with learning disabilities. Smith and Brown (1989) suggest that:

> Relationships between people who come together on the basis of alienation or a shared history of oppression are complex and ambivalent. People whose identity is fragile are vulnerable to competition and envy and may find it difficult to identify with each other. They see in the stigma of the other their own degradation. (p. 231)

In this way, adults with learning disabilities may internalise the view that their relationships with other residents are unimportant and will therefore gravitate towards staff.

However, natural bonds and friendships can form between adults with learning disabilities. For example, friendships which develop in day centres or colleges are similar to those of people who are not learning disabled. Yet these relationships often are not encouraged within community settings (we discuss this further in Chapter 2). Full community integration means increasing clients' opportunities for developing relationships (in addition to existing relationships with staff or family members), thus avoiding a continuing culture of reinforced dependency (Smith and Brown, 1989). Clients need to be encouraged to access community resources – for example, sports facilities, adult training colleges and employment – in order to expand their social networks.

The attitudes of the wider community (in addition to the characteristics of learning disabilities *per se*) can be seen as partly responsible for creating clients' strong dependency on their carers. Societal views on what is appropriate, or inappropriate, for people with learning disabilities can make us forget that the clients themselves may have views about their own lives. More attention needs to be paid to what people with learning disabilities have to say about their own experiences – for example, what aspects of their lives lead to feelings of joy, fulfilment, distress or unhappiness.

Part of the impetus behind our research study and the writing of this book was to allow the voices of people with learning disabilities to be heard. All too often studies rely only on third-party information, that is, the views of carers and families, rather than those of the clients themselves. However, people with learning disabilities can speak for themselves and surely have important things to say; it is up to all of us to make sure that we listen. This book is based on research which principally aimed at finding out about clients' experiences of

their relationships with care staff and their feelings about
the endings of these relationships. We hoped that the
research would provide a forum for clients, as well as
care staff, to tell their own stories.

A Note on Terminology

Few groups of people have been given so many different
labels as people with learning disabilities. A label once
considered acceptable comes to be seen as pejorative or
inaccurate, only to be replaced by a series of others
(Sinason, 1992). In this book we use the term 'learning
disabilities', which is widely used in the UK today
(Department of Health, 1991). We recognise, however,
that other alternatives, such as 'learning difficulty' and
'intellectual disability', are frequently used. It is also
worth noting that many of the clients we interviewed
used the older term 'handicapped' in relation to themselves.

Services for people with learning disabilities have
adopted the terms 'clients', 'residents' or 'service users'
to refer to those receiving services. As this book is
primarily concerned with people in residential settings,
we use the terms 'clients' and 'residents' interchangeably.

'Keyworker' is the term usually used for a member of
paid staff (often untrained) who has overall responsibility for the care of a particular client. The nature of a
keyworker's role or responsibilities will vary between
settings (an issue which is discussed in this book), but
generally the keyworker is assigned to the general care
and support of the client. This encompasses working
individually with the client, attending reviews, having
contact with families, coordinating day services and
taking overall responsibility for the client's care plan.
'Staff' and 'keyworker' are used here interchangeably to
refer to carers in residential settings.

We have tried to avoid sexist language. Because of the awkwardness of repeatedly stating 'he or she' or 'his or her', we have opted to use the feminine pronoun to refer to unspecified clients or keyworkers. We felt this was appropriate, as the majority of clients and staff who participated in our study were women.

All names of clients and staff members referred to in the book are pseudonyms. We have also changed any details which could be used to identify individuals, in order to protect their confidentiality.

How the Book is Organised

The main purpose of this book is to describe clients' and staff members' experiences of the keyworking relationship, how these relationships end, and the impact of these endings on clients as well as staff. Ultimately, our aim is to help staff and clients in saying goodbye. We hope that, with a greater understanding of what happens when relationships end, staff will be better equipped to say goodbye to their clients in ways which minimise the emotional upheaval of the separation. To this end, we have developed a set of recommendations for how services can plan for the endings of keyworker relationships.

Chapters 2 and 3 provide the context for the material presented in the later chapters. In Chapter 2 we review the research and theoretical literature relevant to understanding staff–client relationships. This chapter summarises studies of care staff's roles and of the friendship needs of adults with learning disabilities. It also reviews the concepts of attachment, loss and grief, which provide a framework for understanding the difficulties in ending staff–client relationships. In Chapter 3 we outline how we carried out our own research and we discuss its limitations. These two chapters are intended for readers who are interested in the theoretical and methodological background to the book. However, both Chapters 2 and 3 could easily be skipped by readers who are primarily interested in the stories told by clients and staff.

Chapters 4–7 constitute the core of the book. In these chapters we present the themes that emerged from our interviews with clients and staff; we illustrate these themes with extensive quotations from the interviews. Chapter 4 focuses on what the keyworker role is all about: it presents clients' and staff's views of what keyworkers do and the part that keyworkers play in clients' lives. Chapter 5 focuses on how keyworkers leave – that is, how and what clients are told when keyworkers move away; again, clients' and staff's views are presented in turn. Chapter 6 addresses the emotional impact of endings, from the clients' point of view: here clients describe how they have felt after their keyworkers have left. Chapter 7 provides a parallel account of staff's views about the impact of separations: here staff describe how they have felt after leaving posts, as well as how they think their clients may have felt.

Chapters 8 and 9 draw together the clients' and staff's accounts and address their theoretical and practical implications. In Chapter 8 we discuss the themes that emerged from the interviews and relate these to the literature; we aim here to develop an understanding of why it is hard to say goodbye. In Chapter 9 we present a set of recommendations and guidelines to help services plan sensitively for the endings of keyworking relationships. The stories of clients and staff presented in the earlier chapters are used as a foundation for these guidelines.

CHAPTER 2

Literature Review

The problem of staffing residential facilities is not new. Services for people with learning disabilities have a long history of recruitment and retention difficulties (Allen et al., 1990). In the early nineteenth century, with the opening of the first mental handicap institution at Adenberg, the staffing situation became so bad that it was later to be described as having been run by 'two uneducated peasants' (Kanner, 1964). More recently, in the early 1970s, a British hospital ward for 20 children with severe learning disabilities was reported to have had 89 members of nursing staff over a three-year period (Stephen and Robertson, 1972, as cited in Clegg and Landsdall-Welfare, 1995). Although recent service developments have decreased the rate of staff turnover, it is estimated that about a quarter of community residential staff leave their posts every year (Allen et al., 1990). This means that clients can face multiple changes of care staff, sometimes over short periods of time. How does this unstable staffing situation of residential services impact on people with learning disabilities who have spent most of their lives in institutional care?

The issue of staff turnover is critical to clients' welfare, but has been addressed only briefly in the literature (for example, Zaharia and Baumeister, 1978; George and Baumeister, 1981; Allen et al., 1990). These studies have focused mainly on measures of staff stress and job satisfaction. Certain factors have been found to be associated with staff leaving posts, including lack of

integration of staff members, low pay, and lack of
training and support systems to deal with the behavioural difficulties of clients. Allen et al. (1990) compared
staff working in a long-stay hospital with those working
in new local authority community housing. Surprisingly,
the closing institution was found to have greater staff
stability than the developing community service. For
staff working in the community, role ambiguity was
found to be the factor most closely linked to the propen-
sity to leave; that is, staff who were more uncertain about
their roles were more likely to leave.

It is, of course, inevitable that some staff will move
on. However, as Clegg and Lansdall-Welfare (1995)
have pointed out, the clients' needs for support must
take priority when the person who has worked with
them is leaving. A few studies have pointed to the difficulties arising for clients following the unexpected loss
of significant relationships with others. For example,
Harper and Wadsworth (1993) noted that loss may lead
to depression, behavioural problems and psychiatric
symptoms. Emerson (1977) estimated that 50 per cent
of crises in the lives of people with learning disabilities
involve the loss of a close relationship. Clinical case
studies, such as Sinason's (1992) well-known account of
a young woman called 'Maureen', have vividly
described the cycle of upheaval and despair that can
occur when staff members leave, and how the sensitivity
of a keyworker can help the client to recover and move
on. Clearly, staff departures can be a significant event in
clients' lives. Yet there is a dearth of research invest-
igating this in any depth, and (as far as we are aware) no
previous research has attempted to study this from the
client's point of view.

This chapter reviews some theoretical literature, as
well as the small body of research studies, which throw
light on how staff departures can affect clients living in
residential care. The chapter addresses two main areas:

the role of care staff in the lives of people with learning disabilities, and the endings of staff–client relationships. It draws on the concepts of attachment and loss to provide a framework for understanding the nature of clients' relationships with care staff and how clients might react to the endings of these relationships.

The Meaning of Staff–Client Relationships

What roles do care staff in residential settings play in the lives of people with learning disabilities? How do staff themselves perceive their roles, and how do the residents perceive them? How can we make sense of the close relationships that sometimes develop between clients and staff?

The role of care staff
The daily contact of staff is central to both the emotional development and the socialisation of residents (Hastings and Remmington, 1994). Staff behaviour has been studied for this reason, especially the interactions between staff and clients (Clegg et al., 1991; Felce et al., 1991; Clegg, Standen and Jones, 1996). The degree of learning disability obviously determines, in part, the work of the staff member. When the resident has a profound learning disability, for example, caring may involve considerable amounts of physical support. It can involve lifting, washing and dressing the person, dealing with incontinence, and feeding and caring for the person throughout the day. Most carers of people with learning disabilities, however, describe physical care as relatively untaxing (Twigg and Atkin, 1994). The impact of behavioural problems is often perceived as much more stressful. Generally the staff face a very demanding role, and often with minimal support.

In their study of changing residential services for adults with learning disabilities, Allen et al. (1990)

explored nursing staff's perceptions of the nature of their work and their roles. One question asked of the staff was whether they saw their job as most similar to the role of a nurse, teacher or carer. They gave a great diversity of responses, which seemed to depend at least partly on their level of qualifications. Interestingly, however, the qualified nursing staff indicated uncertainty about whether the term 'nurse' provided an appropriate description of their role. Fewer than half used only the term 'nurse' to describe their role, over a third avoided the term altogether, and the rest described their job as a mixed role; only a minority used the term 'carer'. Allen et al. conclude that most qualified nursing staff saw their job in complex ways, and not simply as 'normal nursing'.

A study by Clegg et al. (1996) offers a more in-depth picture of how care staff view their roles and their relationships with clients. Clegg and colleagues interviewed staff members from four residential units for adults with profound learning disabilities, and asked them to describe their relationship with a particular client. Four types of relationship were identified. The 'provider' relationship focused on meeting the client's basic care needs; the emphasis was on the staff member's physical and practical support for the resident with the activities of daily life. The 'meaning maker' relationship was characterised by the staff's efforts to engage with and understand the client; this often involved trying to make sense of the client's limited communication. The 'mutual' relationship was characterised by shared joy concerning the client's development. Finally, the 'companion' relationship was described as more of a friendship, which evolved with trust and emotional comfort.

Perhaps not surprisingly, the clients' level of disability was related to the type of relationship which the staff developed with them. Staff tended to have 'provider' and 'meaning maker' relationships with the more disabled clients; 'mutual' and 'companion' relationships were more likely with the more able clients. Staff also described the latter two types of relationship as more satisfying and enjoyable. The 'provider' relationship, which was described as least satisfying, was seen by some staff as a temporary stage prior to developing a more interactive relationship. Interestingly, this study also found that the keyworking relationship worked least well for residents in settings which had high staff turnover and few staff with vocational qualifications.

The findings of this study are informative in illustrating the variety of forms which staff–client relationships can take. Clearly, care staff develop different types of relationships with different clients, and some of these relationships can become close and mutually satisfying. However, Clegg et al.'s study examined staff–client relationships only from the perspective of the staff, and thus leaves open the question of how the clients themselves experience their relationships with care workers.

Clients' relationships with care staff may take on particular importance for those who have few, or no, other close relationships. This issue has not been examined directly in studies of people with learning disabilities, but it has been addressed in a study of support for institutionalised older adults. Powers (1992) compared residents who had well-integrated social networks with those who had very limited relationships and spent most of their time at home. The roles and relationships with staff differed for these two groups. Clients who had wider social networks relied heavily on their own resources and social contacts, with staff offering minimal direct care and support. In contrast, residents who were lacking in wider social relationships were much more reliant on staff, and seemed to become increasingly isolated and depressed. In other words, the residents' social networks appeared to play a part in shaping the staff's roles. Some parallels can be drawn here to people with learning disabilities, who often have few relationships outside of the residential setting. In the absence of other relationships, care staff are likely to become a central part of clients' lives. The limited social networks of many adults with learning disabilities is an issue we turn to next.

The friendship needs of people with learning disabilities
Several writers have expressed concern about the paucity of friendships and close relationships experienced by many people with learning disabilities living in the community (for example, Atkinson, 1989; Flynn, 1989; Firth and Rapley, 1990; Chappell, 1994). A substantial number of adults, whether living with family or in residential establishments, seem to lack close friends altogether. Such restricted social relationships can lead to a deep sense of loneliness, isolation and exclusion. A comprehensive review of the social behaviour of people with learning disabilities concluded that friendships are among the most valued aspects of their lives (Landesman-Dwyer and Berkson, 1984). Interestingly, several studies described in this review suggested that people living in larger residences had more friendships, whilst people living in smaller community residences experienced greater isolation and greater dependency on paid staff.

Drawing on a social theory of disability, Chappell (1994) proposes several reasons for clients' lack of friendships and for the failure of community care to increase clients' social networks. She argues that there are both ideological and practical constraints on adults with learning disabilities which can make it difficult for them to make friendships.

Chappell suggests that one underlying assumption behind the philosophy of normalisation (discussed in Chapter 1) is that relationships between disabled people are less valuable than relationships with non-disabled people. The argument is that by associating with each other, people with learning disabilities (who are already stigmatised by society) will feel even more stigmatised. Normalisation has been concerned with social integration into the non-disabled community, which has taken precedence over social relationships between disabled people themselves. In this way, normalisation has limited clients' opportunities for developing friendships with each other. Chappell argues, however, that one type of relationship should not be considered more valuable than another. People with learning disabilities can create bonds with each other, based on shared life experiences or common interests, which may lead to close friendships. Most importantly, Chappell suggests that adults with learning disabilities, like all other adults, must be allowed to have a choice about who they want to be friends with.

Chappell also identifies some financial and environmental constraints, implicit to the organisation of services, which can hinder the development of friendships for adults with learning disabilities and reinforce their dependency and isolation. For example, clients often have restricted access to their own money (and generally have a low income anyway), which can prevent their participation in social activities, such as buying drinks for friends in the pub, going to the cinema, or eating out. Staffing arrangements may mean that clients do not have access to support from a carer to go out in the evenings, or there may only be sufficient staff for large groups of clients to go out together. How can people have any choice over their relationships with others if they are either denied opportunities for going out at all, or always grouped together with clients who may have different interests and different needs from themselves? There may also be a lack of space or privacy for clients in the home environment, which can make it almost impossible for clients to have opportunities for intimacy with others in their own homes.

Social skills training is often seen by services as the solution to clients' lack of relationships (Chappell, 1994). Although such training can be effective and helpful (Firth and Rapley, 1990), social skills will be of little use if people are not given the opportunities to establish relationships with others. As Firth and Rapley (1990) point out, a critical role for staff is to make such opportunities available and to support clients when they begin to develop friendships. If relationships between people with learning disabilities are respected, and if clients are allowed to make choices about who they spend time with, then ultimately they may be able to develop more satisfying social relationships and become less dependent on paid staff.

Implications for staff–client relationships

Given the paucity of relationships experienced by many people with learning disabilities, it is not surprising that residents may interpret their relationships with staff members as friendships (Firth, 1986). Such relationships may meet their needs for a close emotional attachment in the absence of anyone else in their lives with whom intimate feelings can be exchanged. In some situations there may be a genuine commitment on the part of residents and staff which lasts beyond the end of the keyworking relationship. However, the nature of these relationships is not always clear to either party, and each may have a different perception of it. This can cause great distress and loss if the worker moves away, or if the client has perceived the relationship as a friendship, but this has not been understood by the staff member (Firth and Rapley, 1990).

In a study of relationships between social workers and people with learning disabilities, Atkinson (1989) identified the discomfort and ambivalence experienced by professionals when clients appear to become over-dependent on them. The professional can feel 'drawn in' by the client's needs. Atkinson argues that it is important for professionals themselves to understand the nature of such relationships, and to talk with clients about their working relationship in order to clarify misunderstandings and avoid raising false expectations which may ultimately cause greater distress.

Atkinson's study points to the importance of staff having a clear and realistic idea about the nature (and limitations) of their roles. If a keyworker feels that a client's welfare rests entirely upon her shoulders, she may end up feeling overwhelmed by the client's dependency and by her own responsibilities. Eventually, escape from the relationship may feel the only available coping strategy for the keyworker. Such a cycle of involvement and rejection is common in services for people with learning disabilities and can lead to greater harm by increasing the client's insecurity. These issues are considered further, in the context of attachment theory, below.

Attachment theory: a framework for understanding staff–client relationships
Attachment theory (Bowlby, 1969, 1988) provides a useful framework for thinking about relationships, particularly those in which one person is providing help or care for another. According to Bowlby, human beings are fundamentally relationship-seeking: they have an innate tendency to develop strong bonds to other individuals. Bowlby proposed that the quality of infants' bonds with their parents or other significant caregivers will influence the quality of their relationships later in life. When a caregiver is emotionally responsive and reliable, the child forms a 'secure attachment', which provides a safe base from which the child can explore the world and eventually develop new relationships. In contrast, an 'anxious attachment',

caused by unresponsive or inconsistent caregiving, can
lead to unfulfilled needs for nurturance and difficulties
in relationships later on. Bowlby also suggested that, on
the basis of early experiences, individuals develop
'internal working models' of relationships – that is, a set
of beliefs and expectations about their interactions with
other people. For example, an individual may come to
believe that no one will love her unless she always shows
a smiling face. In other words, previous relationships
will influence the individual's later expectations about
the availability and responsiveness of close others.

Attachment theory has been criticised as having a
number of limitations (see Dunn, 1993, for a critique).
For example, it has over-emphasised the role of
mothers, paying little, if any, attention to fathers and
other caregivers; it has not addressed the role of social
stresses on primary carers; and it has tended to patholo-
gise parent–child dyads in which there are attachment
difficulties. While these criticisms are important and
well-founded, they do not weaken the fundamental
thesis that the history of caregiving which a child
receives will play a role in how that individual relates to
others later in life. Our early relationships with others
will affect, for example, whether we feel that others can
be trusted and depended on, and how comfortable we
feel with closeness and intimacy.

How can attachment theory help to shed light on the
relationships between adults with learning disabilities
and care staff? First of all, it can help us understand why
people with learning disabilities are particularly likely to
have difficulties with establishing and maintaining relationships. As Clegg and Lansdall-Welfare (1995) argue,
learning disabilities can make parent–infant bonding
difficult. A variety of factors may influence the attitudes
of parents towards their disabled child, such as the
severity of the disability, the presence of additional
illnesses, and the way in which the news of the disability

is given (Gallimore et al., 1989; Goldberg et al., 1995).
Although some parents will have positive attitudes,
others will have difficulties in bonding which 'will result
in a sizeable group of insecure children' (Clegg and
Lansdall-Welfare, 1995, p. 298). Furthermore, a history
of institutional or residential care, commonly characterised by unstable staffing, is unlikely to facilitate
secure attachments. As Gallimore et al. (1989) have
suggested, a cycle of rejection is often experienced by
children with learning disabilities, which is likely to
result in increased insecurity and continuing difficulties
with forming attachments in later life.

Clients' attachment histories can help us to make
sense of problematic behaviours – such as 'clinginess',
demanding behaviour, or withdrawal – which can occur
in clients' interactions with staff. Attachment research
suggests that children who lack secure attachments will
have later difficulties in their interactions with others.
For example, attachment style at one year of age has
been shown to predict children's ability to interact with
peers and teachers when they start school: children with
a history of insecure attachments are more likely to cling
to their teachers, to be introverted, and to have unpro-
voked aggressive outbursts (Bretherton, 1991). Drawing
on such research, Clegg and Lansdall-Welfare (1995)
describe how they used attachment theory to make sense
of difficulties in the relationships between three adults
with learning disabilities and their care workers. For
example, one client was referred for help because of
increasing aggressive behaviour towards others when his
favourite day centre worker spent time with anyone else.
Staff initially construed this behaviour as 'attention-
seeking', but a closer analysis, which took into account
the client's previous relationships with his family and
care workers, suggested a much more complex picture of
his dependency on, and anxiety about, caregivers. Clegg
and Lansdall-Welfare describe how work with the care

staff, focused on developing an understanding of the client's behaviour, can help to resolve difficulties such as these which often arise in staff–client relationships.

Finally, attachment theory suggests that caregivers' own experiences of being cared for will affect how they provide care to others. That is, the quality of staff's own early attachments may influence their ability to be attuned to, and respond sensitively to, their clients. Research evidence from the mental health field lends some support to this idea. For example, Dozier, Cue and Barnett (1994) investigated how case managers responded to patients suffering from serious psychological disorders, and found that case managers with secure attachment styles were more able to respond to the patients' underlying needs. A more recent study, examining how student therapists responded to role-played clients on a video, found a link between attachment and empathy: student therapists with more secure attachment styles tended to respond more empathically to clients' statements (Rubino et al., in press). These studies have important implications for those involved in caring for clients. Care staff need to be aware of how their personal histories can play a role in their feelings towards, and responses to, clients. Supervision can help staff to explore these issues and make sense of their reactions to clients, so that ultimately they can respond sensitively and appropriately to their clients' needs.

The Ending of Staff–Client Relationships

The loss of relationships is a frequent occurrence in residential care settings. As we have already noted, care staff often do not stay long in any one job, which means that residents regularly face the loss of someone who has been intimately involved in their lives. Residents themselves are sometimes moved from one residential setting to another, leaving their few friends or acquaintances behind. Separation and loss can thus become central features of life for adults with learning disabilities. What does the literature tell us about how the loss of relationships may affect clients?

The impact of separation and loss
According to Bowlby (1973), experiences of separation and loss, and threats of being abandoned, constitute a large proportion of the major stressors faced by all human beings. That is, the disruption or ending of a close relationship, whether brought about by separation or death, typically arouses strong feelings of distress and anxiety. Bowlby observed the distress that occurred when normal infants and children were separated from their mother or primary caregiver. He noted that even brief separations aroused intense responses in the children, including despair, anger, anxiety and withdrawal. These responses are part of the normal process of grieving, that is, how all human beings react to death or personal loss. In this way, the ending of a resident's relationship with a keyworker can be understood in terms of normal loss and grief.

While separation and loss are distressing for all of us, attachment theory suggests that these experiences will be even more difficult for people who do not have a history of secure attachments (Bowlby, 1973). Individuals who have had unresponsive or inconsistent caregiving are more likely to have greater fears of separation and to be more sensitive to loss. For these individuals, normal grief reactions may take a more exaggerated or extreme form.

Strong reactions to separation and loss have been noted by observers of children in residential care, who typically have a history of insecure attachments. For example, Swanson and Schaefer (1988) describe the variety of reactions children have after being placed in residential treatment. Some present as cold and aloof, seeming to protect themselves from another rejection by refusing to get involved with new caregivers. Others may be extremely compliant, seeming determined to please others in an effort to avoid being sent away again. Still others may behave immaturely, regressing to behaviour characteristic of younger children, perhaps in an effort to elicit emotional nurturance from the new caregivers. Swanson and Schaefer note that although different children may express their feelings in a variety of ways, their histories of poor attachments make them acutely sensitive to experiences of separation. Lanyado (1989) also comments on separation and loss in residential work with disturbed children. She describes how children can experience the change of care workers as a devastating rejection, which can precipitate aggressive and self-destructive behaviour. Because of many previous losses, these children have difficulty in coping with yet another change in caregiver.

In summary, Bowlby's framework for understanding separation and loss, and observations of children in residential care, can shed some light on the potential impact of changes in care staff for people with learning disabilities. The loss of any significant caregiving relationship is likely to lead to a process of grieving. For many adults with learning disabilities, who have an impoverished history of care – usually involving repeated losses of caregivers – the departure of a keyworker may be felt even more acutely. We now turn to the small body of literature which has addressed the issue of loss specifically in relation to people with learning disabilities.

Loss in the lives of people with learning disabilities
Although no previous research studies have examined how residents respond to loss when care staff leave, some studies have looked more generally at loss and bereavement in the lives of people with learning disabilities. However, the research is relatively sparse, in

contrast to the large body of research on grief and bereavement in the general (non-disabled) population.

Historically it has been assumed that people with learning disabilities do not have the capacity to form strong emotional bonds and intimate relationships that could culminate in feelings of personal loss, and therefore that they do not experience grief (Oswin, 1981; Yanok and Beifus, 1993). It is not surprising, therefore, that grief reactions have frequently gone unnoticed or have been mislabelled by care staff (Harper and Wadsworth, 1993). In more recent years, however, there has been a growing recognition that bereavement and grief are important areas to address, and that clients need appropriate support when they are bereaved (for example, Oswin, 1981, 1991; Wadsworth and Harper, 1991; James, 1995).

Emerson (1977) was instrumental in highlighting the impact of bereavement on the emotional lives of people with learning disabilities. In her clinical consultancy role to emotionally disturbed learning-disabled adults, Emerson reported frequent contacts by group homes or institutions because a client who had previously shown few problems had suddenly 'for no apparent reason' started presenting emotional and management difficulties. The symptoms included verbal and physical aggression, and extreme withdrawal. Using crisis intervention approaches to identify the precipitating stressor, Emerson found that in half of the referred cases the death or loss of someone close had occurred. Typically, however, care workers did not recognise the emotional significance of the loss and did not respond appropriately to the client after the event. There seemed to be little support for the client's emotional reactions, and little time for facilitating adjustment to the changes in the client's life.

Several other studies have suggested that clients' reactions to loss may go unrecognised and consequently develop into behavioural or emotional problems, which may eventually lead to referrals to specialist services. For example, a study by Ghazziudin (1988) explored the role of life events in the development of psychiatric disorders in people with learning disabilities. Grief and reactions to the loss of relationships were identified as significant precipitants of psychiatric disorders and behavioural difficulties. Ghazziudin suggests that the clients' symptoms were often viewed in isolation and the effects of their broader life situation, such as the loss of relationships, were not recognised. Similarly, Strachan (1981) noted that nurses working in an institutional setting frequently missed signs of grief and mourning in residents who had been bereaved. Although the nurses showed some understanding of common responses to bereavement, their observations of clients in their care was typically 'no response to the death'.

Harper and Wadsworth (1993) surveyed care staff of adults with moderate to severe learning disabilities about their views of how clients respond to bereavement or loss. This study was unusual in that it also included interviews with clients about the types of losses they had experienced as well as their reactions to those losses. One of the main findings of the study was that people with learning disabilities show a range of grief reactions, which are broadly similar to those of non-disabled adults. These reactions included a mixture of sadness, anger, anxiety, confusion and physical pain. Harper and Wadsworth suggest that these are manifestations of a situational depressive response, which is a normal reaction to personal loss.

Harper and Wadsworth (1993) also suggest that, for a significant minority of clients, grief reactions can become 'dysfunctional'. For example, sadness or anger may become intensified and may be expressed by more extreme behaviours, such as self-injury, passivity, with-drawal, or extreme aggression. Again, parallels can be drawn with non-disabled people: dysfunctional or abnormal grief reactions are known to occur in people without cognitive or developmental impairments (Parkes, 1972; Bowlby, 1980). However, as Harper and Wadsworth point out, certain factors make coping with bereavement more difficult for adults with learning disabilities. First, as we have already noted, care staff often fail to recognise clients' grief. This increases the likelihood that clients will suffer additional emotional distress and develop more serious problems in the aftermath of loss. Second, intellectual impairments and communication problems can complicate the grieving process. Clients with moderate or severe learning disabilities may have difficulties in understanding the permanence of loss, may find it more difficult to adapt to change, and may not be able to express their emotions verbally. Those clients who have difficulty with verbal communication will often express their distress through more concrete behaviours, such as hitting out or withdrawing.

Oswin (1981) suggests that many of the difficulties encountered by people with learning disabilities arise because they are treated differently from the 'normal' population; as a result their needs are not met at crucial periods in their lives, such as at times of bereavement. Clients may be prohibited from expressing and coping with grief by well-intentioned carers who wish to spare the individuals from 'upsetting events' (Seltzer, 1985). Displays of grief are often misinterpreted and thus discouraged, particularly when the emotional and behavioural manifestations are intense or disruptive. Furthermore, symptoms of grief are often treated inappropriately with medication (Day, 1985; Wadsworth and Harper, 1991). As a result, clients are not given the opportunity to learn new coping skills, and are therefore more likely to show dysfunctional grief reactions when faced with new losses (Harper and Wadsworth, 1993).

In summary, people with learning disabilities, like people without disabilities, show a variety of grief reactions in the face of bereavement and loss. Further research is needed to determine those factors which contribute to successful coping (Harper and Wadsworth, 1993). It seems clear, however, that the grieving process is often inhibited by carers' failure to recognise, or to facilitate the expression of, clients' feelings about loss. As a result, clients may experience prolonged emotional turmoil and present with persistent behavioural difficulties. How care staff can help clients adjust to loss is an area which we turn to next.

Helping clients adjust to separation and loss
What can care workers do to help adults with learning disabilities cope with the loss of an important person in their life? Again, there is only a small body of literature which directly addresses this issue. Although the literature focuses on the situation of bereavement, many of the ideas can be applied to the situation of staff departures and the endings of staff–client relationships. We briefly review these ideas below, and also draw more broadly on some literature addressing separation and endings in therapeutic relationships.

Two tasks seem fundamental to helping clients adjust to loss. The first is to be aware of and to recognise potential reactions to loss. The second is to assist with, or facilitate, the grieving process (Oswin, 1981, 1991; Harper and Wadsworth, 1993; James, 1995). These tasks can pose some special difficulties for staff working with clients who have moderate or severe learning disabilities.

As we have already noted, it can be particularly difficult for staff to recognise clients' reactions to loss when grief is not expressed verbally, but through disruptive or challenging behaviours. Sinason (1992) urges care staff and clinicians to pay greater attention to the meaning of clients' behaviour: 'If we do not try to make sense of behaviours such as head banging and self injury, we can be accused of joining in the conspiracy of silence' (p. 223). Becoming aware of the feelings behind clients' behaviours is a crucial first step in being able to offer help. When an important relationship has ended for a client, whether through death or separation, it is imperative for staff to try to understand the personal meaning of the loss for the individual. There is also a need for further research exploring the experience of loss for people with learning disabilities, in order to provide a knowledge base for those involved in clients' care.

The second task – assisting in the grieving process – involves helping clients to recognise, label and express their feelings. Oswin (1991) has written about how staff can guide and support the grieving process by putting clients' feelings into words, exploring the meaning of the loss with clients, and giving them the opportunity to ventilate intense feelings. Such an approach can be used effectively with clients who have limited verbal expressive skills, although of course the communication strategies used will vary depending on the nature and extent of the disability (Oswin, 1991; Harper and Wadsworth, 1993).

Recognising clients' reactions to loss and assisting with the grieving process are issues which apply not only to bereavement, but also to the endings of staff–client relationships. However, the situation of staff departures raises an additional issue, that of preparing the client for separation and loss.

The importance of preparing clients for the endings of their relationships with staff has long been recognised in the psychotherapy literature (for example, Weiner, 1975). Although clearly there are differences between psychotherapy and caring for clients in residential care, important similarities also exist: both situations involve emotional support and the development of a close relationship between client and helper. In situations of this kind, preparation can ease the pain of ending, as Weiner points out:

> the terminal phase of psychotherapy is a period of separation for the patient, often mourned in the same way as other separations from familiar people, places, and activities are mourned. The pain of such separations tends to be eased by opportunities to prepare for them, especially if feelings about the separation can be aired and worked through before it becomes final. (Weiner, 1975, p. 281).

Weiner points out that if the therapist ends the relationship suddenly, with little or no time for discussion, the client may wonder about the motives behind the therapist's behaviour. Clients may feel that they themselves are responsible – for example, that they have done something 'bad' to cause the therapist to leave. Siebold (1991), also writing on termination in psychotherapy, urges therapists to give clients 'sufficient facts so they can master the news, and then to allow them as much time as possible to process this information' (p. 194). Although the loss of an important relationship may never be painless, such preparation can help clients adjust to the loss and cope with future losses more effectively.

Care workers' own feelings of loss may get in the way of preparing their clients for separation. As Rosenberg (1990) points out, the endings of staff–client relationships can affect not only the clients, but the staff as well:

> When we work with disabled clients, we naturally become attached. We care not only for them but about them. Our work requires that we form attachments for brief periods of time and then let them go ... we find ourselves suddenly separated from people we have grown to care about. (p. 76)

Care staff are repeatedly faced with having to let go of clients they have become attached to and begin the helping process all over again with new clients. Rosenberg argues that staff themselves need support and time for grieving over lost relationships with clients. If staff are not allowed to acknowledge their own feelings of loss, it can be difficult for them to allow their clients to express feelings of loss (Swanson and Schaefer, 1988). Furthermore, if staff are not given time to grieve, they may find it difficult to start and maintain new relationships with clients.

Summary

The relationships between adults with learning disabilities and care staff have not been studied extensively. The few existing studies suggest that these relationships are often complex, involving more than physical or practical care. Care staff may play a central role in the lives of clients who have few other close relationships. Some staff–client relationships can become close and mutually satisfying; however, staff may also become uncomfortable with their clients' dependency. Attachment theory can help us to understand the relationships between clients and care staff, in particular the difficulties that adults with learning disabilities may have in establishing relationships and the problematic behaviours that can occur in their interactions with staff.

Although no previous studies have examined how clients react to the departures of care staff, the literature on bereavement and loss suggests that the endings of such relationships can be very distressing. The loss of any important relationship, whether through death or separation, is likely to lead to a process of grieving. When faced with bereavement, people with learning disabilities show a variety of grief reactions which are broadly similar to those of non-disabled adults. Clients who have a history of loss or rejection are likely to be more sensitive to further losses, and their grief reactions may take a more extreme form. However, those who care for adults with learning disabilities may not always recognise their expressions of grief. This can complicate the grieving process, leading to prolonged emotional turmoil and behavioural problems.

There is clearly a need for research to examine in greater depth how adults with learning disabilities and care staff perceive their relationships, and how the endings of these relationships affect clients. The literature on bereavement and loss provides some clues about the significant impact that staff departures may have, but research addressing this directly is lacking. Furthermore, the available research tells us little about how clients themselves feel about their relationships with care staff and what happens when staff leave. In the next chapter, we describe our own research study, which aimed to examine the endings of staff–client relationships from the perspectives of both clients and staff.

CHAPTER 3

How the Research was Conducted

Our research study had two broad aims. Most importantly, we wanted to find out about residents' experiences and views of the keyworking relationship, and in particular, how they felt about relationships that had ended. Secondly, we wanted to find out about staff's experiences and views on this same subject. To get this information, we carried out separate, semi-structured interviews with 12 residents and 18 staff. The qualitative data obtained from the interviews were then analysed, drawing on procedures from the grounded theory approach (described later in this chapter).

For the sake of clarity, we will describe the research as two parallel studies: the resident study and the staff study. A set of research questions provided the structure for each study. For the resident study, these were:

1. How do residents experience and describe their relationships with keyworkers?
2. How do residents recall the process of ending previous relationships with keyworkers?
3. What were residents' feelings about separations for keyworkers?

A parallel set of questions underpinned the staff study:

1. How do staff describe their relationships and interactions with residents?
2. How did staff prepare clients for when they left?

3. What were the staff members' feelings about ending relationships with residents?
4. How do staff conceptualise the potential impact of the leaving process on residents?

Both residents and staff were asked to talk retrospectively about their experiences. Due to our own time limitations, we were unable to interview participants immediately before a separation and then follow them up after the separation occurred. Nor were we able to interview resident–staff pairs, that is, to talk to a resident and her previous keyworker about their mutual experiences of ending their relationship. (The logistical problems in doing this proved too great, as the keyworkers had moved on to other jobs.) Given these limitations, the research provides a kind of 'snapshot' view of residents' and staff's experiences.

The participants in the resident and staff studies were recruited from residential services for adults with learning disabilities in an outer London borough. Some of these services were run by the local authority, while others were voluntary-sector organisations. Before beginning the research, we obtained ethical approval from the local research ethics committee.

In this chapter we present a summary of who participated in the research and the methods and procedures we used to gather our data. The method of analysing the data is then summarised, followed by a brief discussion of the methodological limitations of the research.

THE RESIDENT STUDY

Participants

All residents who participated in the research were living in 24-hour staffed community homes. Residents had to meet 3 criteria in order to be included in the study:

1. To be able to give informed consent to participate
2. To be able to communicate verbally
3. To have had experience of a previous keyworking relationship which had ended because the keyworker had left the service and moved away.

The residents came from 6 different homes (which included a total of 34 residents). We interviewed 15 residents who met the inclusion criteria for the research, but 3 participants had very limited communication and, as a result, their interviews were not able to be used in the final analysis of the data.

Characteristics of the residents
Of the 12 residents, 7 were women and 5 were men. They ranged in age from 34 to 72 years, with an average age of 44. The ethnicity of all participants was identified by staff as White British. Staff in the homes indicated that the participants had a range of learning disabilities – 4 participants had a diagnosis of Down's syndrome; 2 had a diagnosis of cerebral palsy; 2 were described as having physical and learning disabilities (both wheelchair users); and 4 were described as having a general learning disability (for the latter 2 groups, no known diagnosis was identified). We asked keyworkers to fill out the Degree of Dependency Rating Scale (Kushlick et al., 1973), to give us some idea of each client's capacities and behaviour. Most of the participants were described by their keyworkers as having a low level of dependency.

The participants had been living in their current residential units for an average of 5 years (the length of time ranged from 1.5 to 7 years); 5 participants had resided in long-stay hospital or institutional care since childhood, and 7 participants had grown up with their families. A review of information about residents' daily activities indicated that 7 participants attended day centres, 3 participants worked in sheltered employment placements, and 2 combined working and attending a day centre.

Procedure

Before interviewing each resident, we met her together with her current keyworker to explain the purpose and procedures of the research. At this stage, consent to participate in the study and permission to tape-record the interviews were requested. Written consent was obtained first from the resident and then from the keyworker (on behalf of the resident). Once a resident had agreed to participate, we spent some time with her alone, as an opportunity for us to get to know each other, and to address any questions or concerns which may have arisen.

Residents were interviewed on their own, with the exception of 2 residents whose current keyworkers were present in order to facilitate communication. The interviews lasted, on average, about 45 minutes.

The Interview

The interview had a semi-structured format, covering set topics but allowing for flexibility in how and when questions were asked. Residents were asked to think about a keyworker who had worked with them in the past and who had now left. The interview covered the following key areas:

- What do you remember about that keyworker? What kinds of things did you used to do together?
- What happened when your keyworker left?
- How did you feel at that time?

The interview schedule consisted of a set of questions which served as a guide for the interviewer, but not all questions were asked in every interview. The questions evolved over the course of the study: some of the early interviews led us to modify or add to the questions we asked. This approach is in keeping with the grounded theory method (Strauss and Corbin, 1998). The interview schedule, which lists the core questions, is presented in Appendix A.

In conducting the interviews, we drew on guidelines highlighted in the literature on interviewing people with learning disabilities (Sigelman et al., 1981; Flynn, 1986; Chapman and Oakes, 1995). A useful consensus has developed about types of questions, how to ask them, the most appropriate setting for the interview and certain safeguards which can be built into the data collection (Atkinson, 1988). These findings are summarised below.

First, Sigelman et al. (1981) suggest that open-ended questions are more useful, as they avoid problems with acquiescence and over-reporting associated with yes/no questions. Open-ended questions also avoid a reported tendency for people with learning disabilities to display 'recency effects', that is, choosing the second option in either/or questions. Wyngaarden (1981) advocates unthreatening, relaxed, conversational-style interviews, with a preference for individual interviews in order to maintain privacy and confidentiality. Flynn (1986) adds to these suggestions by urging the researcher to check out the respondent's level of communication in advance as far as possible. He also suggests that tape recording interviews can make the procedure seem less test-like. The preferred setting for these interviews seems to be the person's own home (Flynn, 1986), as this may allow for a more relaxed interview process. Finally, Wyngaarden proposes starting with easier questions to establish some rapport, keeping the more difficult or emotional questions until the middle or end of the interview. He suggests beginning with closed questions, and following on with more open questions to assist this process.

These principles were incorporated as much as possible into the process of interviewing the residents.

THE STAFF STUDY

Participants

All staff who participated in the study were working in community homes for people with learning disabilities. Staff had to meet 2 criteria in order to be included in the study:

1. To have had experience of being a keyworker in a residential service
2. To have ended a keyworking relationship with a client (because they had left the service or changed jobs within the service).

The staff came from 11 different homes (5 of these were homes where we also interviewed residents). Of the 21 staff who volunteered to participate, 3 did not meet the criteria for the study. A total of 18 staff were therefore included in the study.

Characteristics of the staff

Of the 18 staff, 11 were women and 7 were men. They ranged in age from 25 to 55 years, with an average age of 33. In terms of ethnicity, 16 described themselves as White British, 1 as Irish, and 1 as Afro-Caribbean. The staff had been working with people with learning disabilities for an average of 8 years (the length of time ranged from 2.5 to 29 years); 10 described themselves as Residential Support/Care Workers, 2 as Senior Care Workers, 3 as Deputy/Assistant Home Managers, and 3 as Home Managers. The vocational and training experiences of staff were quite varied – 6 staff reported receiving 'on-the-job training' and relevant brief courses, 4 had a nursing qualification (Registered Nurse in Mental Handicap), 3 had gained a diploma in social or community care, 1 was a psychology graduate, 2 were in the process of part-time social work training, and 2 had received no training at all.

Characteristics of residents described by staff in the interview
Each staff participant identified a particular client for discussion in the interview. The clients who were discussed consisted of 5 women and 15 men (2 staff chose to talk about 2 clients each). The length of time as keyworker to those clients ranged from 3 months to 6 years, with an average of 2.5 years. The time elapsed since ending the relationship ranged from 1 week to 5 years, with an average of 2 years, and 2 staff had returned to their previous work setting, but with different roles and client responsibilities. Most of the clients discussed in the interviews were described by the staff as having either a low or medium level of dependency, with only 3 being described as high in dependency. (As in the resident study, we asked staff to fill out the Degree of Dependency Rating Scale, to give us some idea of each client's capacities and behaviour.)

Procedure

Staff were interviewed individually in the homes where they worked, at a time when there were enough other staff to cover the shift. All participants gave written consent to participate in the study and permission for us to tape-record the interviews. The interviews lasted approximately 50 minutes.

The Interview

Like the interview for the resident study, the interview with staff followed a semi-structured format. Staff were asked to think about a particular client for whom they had stopped being a keyworker. Usually this meant a client from a previous employment setting (unless the staff member had left and returned to the same service). The interview covered a core set of topics:

- What was your role and relationship with the client?
- What happened when you left your post as keyworker?
- What might have been the impact on the resident of your departure?
- What were your feelings at this time?

As in the resident study, the interview schedule comprised a set of questions which served as a guide, but the structure was flexible in order to allow respondents to describe their experiences in their own way. Again, similar to the resident interview, the questions were modified over the course of the study in order to address emerging issues reported by participants. The staff interview schedule is presented in Appendix B.

The literature on semi-structured interviews informed the way in which we conducted the staff interviews. Burgess (1984) highlights the potential of the semi-structured interview method for gaining access to situations that are otherwise 'closed', or not witnessed by the researcher. A sensitively constructed interview can enable the researcher to understand important phenomena in the participant's own words. Burgess stresses the crucial goal of establishing the trust and confidence of the people who are to be interviewed. The respondent should be allowed to talk freely and with minimal constraint. Burgess also advises the use of an *aide-mémoire* to clarify the agenda with participants and to ensure that similar topics are being addressed in each interview. More specifically, Robson (1993) suggests developing a sequence of questions that should emerge in a logical progression. This sequence allows for more straightforward introductory and descriptive questions at the beginning, followed by the main body of the interview, with more difficult or threatening questions occurring later on. Care needs to be taken at the end of the interview to draw the discussion to a close, sometimes using more straightforward questions to diffuse any possible tension raised by the topics discussed.

The above guidelines provided a useful framework for the staff interviews, allowing each participant to tell her own 'story', whilst also ensuring some consistency in what all participants were asked.

ANALYSIS OF THE DATA

In order to analyse the data obtained from the interviews, the tape-recordings of the interviews were first transcribed verbatim. Two sample transcripts, one of a resident interview and one of a staff interview, are presented in Appendices C and D, respectively. The resident and staff interviews were analysed separately, but in the same way, drawing on procedures from the grounded theory approach. As this approach to qualitative research has been written about extensively elsewhere (for example, Glaser and Strauss, 1967; Charmaz, 1995; Pidgeon and Henwood, 1996; Strauss and Corbin, 1998), we present only a brief description of our procedures, below.

The first stage of analysis was the 'open coding' (Strauss and Corbin, 1998) of the interview transcripts. Each transcript was examined line by line, in order to identify as many different ideas and meanings as possible. Codes were applied to 'chunks' of data of different sizes, ranging from a single word or phrase to one or more sentences (Miles and Huberman, 1994). The aim at this stage was simply to describe the data, rather than to interpret or reduce it. The codes therefore adhered closely to the participants' own words.

In the second stage of analysis, the relationships between different codes, or ideas, were examined. Codes expressing similar meanings were grouped together into categories. A key aspect of the coding procedure (at both this and later stages of the analysis) was the method of 'constant comparison' (Pidgeon and Henwood, 1996). Similarities and differences between concepts, both within and between cases, were noted, to ensure that the complexities and subtleties of the data were explored.

Finally, the relationships between different categories were examined so that similar, or related, categories could be grouped together. This led to the formation of a hierarchical structure of lower- and higher-order categories or themes. During these later stages of the analysis, the codes moved from pure description to include our own interpretations of the data. 'Theoretical memos' (Pidgeon and Henwood, 1996) – that is, ideas and hunches that had been recorded throughout the data collection and initial coding stages – were drawn on to refine the analysis.

During the course of the analysis, we incorporated two procedures to check for, and minimise, any idiosyncrasies or biases in our interpretation of the data. Our aim was to ensure, as far as possible, that our interpretations 'fit' the data. First, another qualitative researcher, who was not part of the project, independently examined a portion of the data and allocated lower-order categories into higher-order themes. There was good agreement between the original analysis and the external researcher's analysis, and the few discrepancies which arose were resolved through discussion. Second, we presented our analysis to a multidisciplinary team working with people with learning disabilities. With the team we discussed the overall findings, how categories were labelled and linked, and how the data related to ideas in the clinical and theoretical literature.

Feedback and ideas from the team were incorporated into the final stages of analysis.

LIMITATIONS OF THE RESEARCH

A central limitation of this research is that only clients with mild learning disabilities were included in the study. Due to the requirements of the interview, one of the criteria for participating in the study was that the residents should have verbal communication skills. Therefore, the residents who participated cannot be considered representative of all people with learning disabilities. Future research could aim to involve a wider range of clients, enabling them to express their views by using symbols, pictures and other communication aids.

A related issue is that, in the staff interviews, most staff chose to talk about clients whose disabilities were in the mild to moderate range (and, in the majority of cases, who had speech). It is possible that the staff focused on more able clients because the endings of these relationships were felt to be easier or more positive. (However, as Chapters 5 and 7 indicate, staff described many of the endings as difficult and upsetting.) Staff who agreed to be interviewed were also a self-selected group and therefore may have differed from those who chose not to participate. For example, participants may have been more reflective or more aware of the emotional aspects of their clients' lives and of the impact of separation. We need to be cautious, therefore, in concluding that the experiences described by the staff in this research are typical of all staff working in the field.

As we mentioned at the beginning of this chapter, another limitation of the research was that both residents and staff were asked to talk retrospectively about their experiences of separation. This meant that we had to rely on their memories of these events; inevitably, in some cases, it may have been difficult for participants to accurately recall the processes and feelings involved. Interviewing residents and staff before and after separations would have given a more accurate picture; it would also have allowed us to compare expectations and anticipations of the event with feelings afterwards.

Because of the design of the research, we were also unable to get residents' and staff's views of the same events. That is, as noted earlier, we could not interview resident–staff pairs because the keyworkers described by the residents had (by definition of the study) moved on to other jobs. Therefore, the research presents residents' and staff's stories about different relationships. Occasionally, however, two staff happened to talk about the same resident (because each had worked in that resident's home), which enabled us to get different staff members' perspectives of the same event. One example of this is Pete's and Debbie's descriptions of Kevin, presented at the beginning of Chapter 1.

Finally, the reliance on interviews as the sole method of data collection raises several issues. We have already noted the problem of excluding clients who have limited verbal communication. However, even more able clients may experience difficulties expressing themselves in a consistent fashion, and may be susceptible to certain 'response sets', such as acquiescence (Chapman and Oakes, 1995). Similarly, the well-documented problem of social desirability (Barker et al., 1994) – that is, interviewees giving answers that they think are expected or acceptable – could also have played a role in the resident and staff interviews, despite our efforts to avoid this. Ideally, future research should supplement interviews with other methods, such as systematic observation of residents' behaviour before and after keyworkers' departures. It would also be useful to ask family members, or other people who know the resident well, about the impact of staff departures: their observations of the leaving process and of the short- and long-term effects would add another perspective.

Although the above limitations must be kept in mind when interpreting the findings of the research, it is also worth noting the benefits of the qualitative interview approach. Qualitative methods allow researchers to compile a fine-grained picture of how people think and feel about experiences or events in their lives. People are allowed to tell their own 'stories', rather than being constrained to answer preformulated questions which may not be relevant to their experience. We hope that our interviews gave both residents and staff a 'voice' to communicate their experiences of separation. While each person's experience may be unique, the themes that emerged from the analysis of the interviews can be used to generate ideas about the leaving process and the impact of staff departures. We hope that these ideas can be followed up and developed, not only by future researchers, but also by people working in the field.

CHAPTER 4

What Keyworkers Do

Jean was the one I could confide in. We got on well together. We used to do what I'm doing now with Pete [current keyworker] you know, going out shopping and other things like that. But I didn't have a calliper, what I have now. But I kept falling over and I needed a lot of support when I went out. And even now I can't go out on my own without staff support, because I might fall over or something like that.

A keyworker is a friend that you can turn to, and it's a friend who I can talk to when I've got problems, like what I'm talking to you about, about what has happened in my life – you know because a lot of things have happened ... They're helpful, so to that end it makes one feel that they are different to all the others and it means that I can turn to them when I've got that many problems or whatever ... It was over a course of time that we got to know each other, and it became hard to undo that relationship ... But it's a question of getting their time and when they're available – which is more important I feel. Like with my present keyworker. It's difficult because I don't know when he's on duty you see.

This was Jim's account of the role of his previous keyworker, Jean. Jim was a 41-year-old man with learning disabilities and physical impairment. He grew up in a long-stay 'mental handicap' hospital where he stayed until his mid-thirties when the hospital closed down. He then lived in a home in the community for three years before moving into his present residential home. At the time of this interview, Jim had been living with 12 other residents for over 2 years.

It was difficult to ascertain a great deal of information about Jim's earlier life from the staff. There was a sense of people not knowing about his history and his life in the institution. Most of our knowledge of Jim's life came from what he told us during the interview and from less formal conversations during our preliminary meetings. Jim explained to us that he had lots of keyworkers throughout his life – both at home and at the day centre. He was very engaging and thoughtful throughout the interview and seemed to value the opportunity to talk about his former life and relationships.

For Jim, and for many of the clients we interviewed, the keyworker encompassed several different roles and relationships. These are described in the first part of this chapter, which presents clients' accounts of the role of the keyworker. The second part of the chapter presents staff's views of the keyworker role, and the third, summary, section brings together the clients' and staff's perspectives.

CLIENTS' ACCOUNTS

Clients' accounts of how they saw their keyworkers fell broadly into three categories: that of provider, nurturer and companion. These are each described in turn. A theme which ran through all the three categories, 'constancy in the lives of clients', is presented at the end.

Provider

Jim was among many clients who described keyworkers as providing help with their practical and physical needs. Within the 'provider' role, keyworkers were seen as recognising clients' primary care needs and their sense of physical dependency on staff. As Jim's description above indicates, he felt he needed to physically lean on his keyworker, Jean.

Many clients we interviewed seemed to have formed a perception of their own dependency, and to have developed a strong reliance on the keyworker for activities of everyday living. In some cases this dependency seemed to be part of a child-like perception of the client looking for an idealised 'parent' figure to take care of her. (This idealised relationship overlapped with other fantasies about the keyworker relationship, described under 'Companion', below.) Audrey, a 28-year-old client who had moderate learning disabilities, hinted at this in her description of a keyworker:

A keyworker is clever, she's nice, she loves me. She does cooking and she helps me on a Saturday.

Audrey had recently lost a keyworker and her present keyworker, Julia, was present throughout the interview, to support Audrey in her communication. Julia explained to us that she herself was leaving in a few weeks and that they had just started to talk about this together.

The view of the keyworker as 'provider' may also reflect a lack of a sense of self-efficacy in some clients, and an uncertainty about their ability to take care of themselves, as Sally's account suggests. Sally, a client of 30 years, was living in a staffed home with 4 other clients. Her keyworker had recently left the home to go travelling around the world and Sally was uncertain about her whereabouts. She lamented the loss of her carer and 'provider':

She bathed and dressed me and now I'm on my own.

In some cases, this reliance on staff suggests the residents' fears about their potential to harm themselves without the supervision of someone in a more 'responsible' role. Guy clearly expressed such feelings in relation to the role of his keyworker:

I feel more relaxed when I have someone to turn to. He looks after me. He has to keep an eye on me.

Guy was a 49-year-old man with mild learning disabilities and a long history of behaviours which challenged services. He had been removed from residential placements in the past, *because I used to break televisions and fire alarms and throw drink at people when I was in [the hospital].* Guy had been living in a staffed home for five years. At the time of our interview, the manager of Guy's home had been seconded to another home for 6 months, and his keyworker was on holiday for a few weeks. Guy named many past keyworkers. He had marks on his face and we were later told that he had the potential to harm himself when things became difficult.

Keyworkers clearly play a central role in helping clients to deal with their everyday lives. Jim perceptively noted, however, that there was a disparity between his own experience of his keyworker and what he thought the keyworker might feel. For Jim, the relationship with the keyworker was a crucial part of his whole world, but he could see that it might be less important for the keyworker, who provided help as part of a job:

But what I'm saying is [for the keyworker], it's their job which is the main thing, isn't it? And their job is to look after the interests of myself ... [For me] it's someone who I can turn to, whereas for the person who is dealing with me, it is a job for them to see that everything is all right, and to see how things are going, and to see about going to reviews whenever they are due, and to meet up with my family.

Nurturer

Clients saw keyworkers as looking after not only their
practical and physical needs, but also their emotional
needs. Their accounts often referred to the nurturing,
calming role of the keyworker, almost as a container for
their anxieties. Sally, for example, expressed her sense of
a very strong connection with her previous keyworker,
Emily. She referred to Emily's capacity to cheer her up
when she was upset or worried:

> *When I was upset and everything went wrong, I used to
> say, 'I'm upset now Emily.' She said 'Why?' I said
> 'Someone has upset me.'*
> Interviewer: And what did she used to do or say?
> *She said 'Come to me Sally, I'll cheer you up.'*
> Interviewer: And how did she do that?
> *Put her arms around me, she said, 'Never mind' ... She
> told me not to worry.*

Molly, a 35-year-old client who was living in a staffed
house with 2 other clients, described not only the
calming influence of her keyworker, Dave, but also
expressed gratitude for his kindness. When we asked her
what happened to her when she was upset, she replied:

> *I get Dave to calm me down ... I'm going to stick with
> Dave because he's nice and he's kind and he's very kind
> to me.*

Like Molly, other clients seemed grateful for any
affection or even the merest hint of tenderness or
kindness. When we asked Audrey what she would miss
about Julia, her keyworker who was about to leave, she
replied: *Julia hugs me. Keyworker looks after me.*
Bill described what he liked about his previous
keyworker: *I liked her when she talked nicely to me in the car*

and all that. For Bill, this kindness seemed new and unusual in his interactions and relationships with others. Apart from fortnightly visits to his father's house, Bill had few social contacts. He was sharing his home with two female residents and one male resident, all of whom had very limited verbal communication. Bill had a lengthy history of residential care in long-stay institutions. He seemed sad and mournful as he reflected on his past life and relationships with those who worked in institutions.

Sadly, these accounts of the importance of being treated 'nicely' and 'kindly' by staff may reflect both the clients' poor sense of self and their history of impoverished care (Bicknell, 1983). It may be difficult for people with disabilities to internalise a stable and positive sense of self in the midst of their vulnerability as receptors of often transitory and insufficient care.

The clients we spoke to were often realistic in acknowledging their dependency on staff. Their awareness of their own needs is reflected in their descriptions of the 'nurturer' and 'provider' roles of staff. Arguably the residents' physical and emotional dependency on staff is reinforced by the setting, wherein people with learning disabilities are often not encouraged to depend on themselves or on each other (Clegg, 1993).

Companion

Nearly all the clients' descriptions of their keyworkers indicated that they saw them as companions or friends. They referred to joint activities and shared interests, as well as simply spending time together talking. Lilly's account of her previous keyworker is typical:

> *I used to have Rosie, and she is very nice – we used to go away on holiday ... I used to go round and see her. She lives round here, but I can't go there now ... Rosie used to dress nice and I liked her. She was nice and she was nice*

*to me, and I was talking to her one day and she would
come in and see me she would.*

Similarly, Nick described going out together regularly
with his keyworker as a companion: *[We] go out for a
drink, go out for a meal, or go up in London somewhere.*
Sometimes keyworkers also seemed to act as a social
link, expanding the clients' social world. That is, they
provided access to wider relationships, outside of the
client's residential home, through their own social
networks. Harry, for example, told us: *He [Harry's
keyworker] takes me out with his friends ... and
[keyworker's] friend took me out for a cup of tea.*
Many accounts suggested that clients saw their
keyworker as different from other staff, and that they
appreciated their unique qualities. When we asked Harry
whether he did anything with his keyworker that he
didn't do with the other staff, he replied: *Talking ... We
talked about what I been doing in the centre.* Nick seemed
to miss the personal attributes of his previous keyworker:

> *I liked his jokes and his company ... I miss his jokes and
> company and drums. I just miss him as a good, good
> keyworker.*

Several clients described their keyworker as 'my best'
or 'closest' friend. There was a depth of feeling in some
of these accounts, suggesting the centrality of the
keyworker in these clients' lives. As Sally put it:

> *Emily was my best friend ... She used to give me things
> like soap. She was very nice. We used to speak about
> everything.*

There is a sense here of staff enabling clients to experience intimacy, otherwise missing in their lives. Such
accounts are consistent with the literature which points

to the paucity of close personal relationships for people with learning disabilities, and the importance of staff as friends, who provide intimacy in isolated lives (Firth and Rapley, 1990).

A few clients referred to their more intense and sometimes sexual feelings towards keyworkers. For example, Audrey said:

I still love him... because he's a nice man, he's good looking. He loves me and I love him.

There may be an element of fantasy about these accounts, where clients seemed to be wishing for more intimate relationships with their keyworkers. Such fantasies might arise out of clients' confusion about the closeness of the keyworking relationship, which may be experienced through the physical and emotional care provided by keyworkers. It is worth noting that the sexual feelings of clients are often feared and repressed in services for people with learning disabilities (Craft and Craft, 1981). Often clients are not encouraged (and are sometimes actively discouraged) to develop relationships even between each other. The expression of intense feelings towards staff, as described above by Audrey and other clients, may arise from attempts to repress their normal, human urges for closeness and intimacy with any other person, including fellow residents.

However, it is also worth pointing out that a few clients indicated their awareness of the very real and obvious boundaries in their relationship with a staff member, as Bill's painful lament suggests: *It wouldn't be allowed if I cuddled her.* Bill's statement seems to reflect his sense of frustration and temptation in the face of his strong feelings for his keyworker.

For some clients, there was an element of reciprocity in how they viewed their relationship with their keyworker. As Jim put it:

We used to get on well together. It was quite a good relationship between the two of us. We got on, we shared our problems out.

Several clients described a mutual experience of giving and receiving care in the keyworking relationship, and almost an equal share of support. Lilly told us:

Yes, we got on together. She looked after me and I looked after her ... I looked after her because she wanted me to, and I sat with her in the dinner hour.

It was difficult to know from these accounts whether the keyworker also viewed the relationship as having elements of reciprocity. As with the accounts of sexual feelings, these descriptions sometimes may have contained an element of fantasy: one of sharing and equality within the relationship, with perhaps a wish to feel needed and to be appreciated for looking after the staff. However, many of the accounts from staff (presented later in this chapter) also indicated a sense of reciprocity and mutuality in the keyworking relationship.

Constancy in the Lives of Clients

As the descriptions above suggest, clients saw their keyworkers in many different ways. But what stands out as a theme running through many of their accounts is a strong sense of their appreciation of the keyworker's constancy: the keyworker was seen as having a long-term perspective on clients' lives and the care they needed. There was a sense of feeling 'known' and understood by the keyworker. In Molly's case, one of her previous keyworkers had instigated her change of placement, rescuing her from a difficult environment and enhancing her quality of life. As Molly explained:

He came to [name of hostel] and he saw me there and he took me here [her current home].

This idea of constancy is crucial for a wider understanding of the importance of stability in the overwhelmingly transient lives of people with learning disabilities. Residents seemed appreciative and grateful for having an attachment with someone who seemed to be 'holding them in mind'. The importance of this constancy is perhaps unsurprising in view of the high staff turnover and transient relationships experienced by many clients living in residential settings (Allen et al., 1990; Clegg and Lansdall-Welfare 1995).

STAFF ACCOUNTS

How can one do justice to the complexity of the keyworker's role? A job? A carer? An advocate? The keyworker spends her time (during the day or through the night) working in the client's home – eating there, sleeping there and spending time with someone who is (in most cases) socially isolated. Clients often have quite limited contact with families and little contact with peers and friends in the community. The keyworker spends intense amounts of time with someone who may have limited communication skills, restricted mobility and a history of deprivation (and often traumatic experiences) in institutional care. The clients may be physically and emotionally dependent on their contacts with staff.

When we asked the group of staff in our study to describe their roles and relationships with clients, they recounted some of the day-to-day aspects of working and caring for adults with learning disabilities living in community homes. Oliver, one of the first keyworkers we interviewed, told us:

Keyworking a client is a piece of work. It's not supposed to be fun. I think I've learnt from Simon [a client] that

you can get emotionally attached and it can be detrimental
to the keyworking job. But that's being a keyworker – it
can be very hands on … I think part of the job is not to
get too attached.

Oliver's story reflects a sense of his own struggle with
the concept of intimacy versus professional distance
from clients. He was unsure about how emotionally
close one should become to clients within the role of
keyworker. At the time of our interview, Oliver had
spent the past four years working in residential care for
people with learning disabilities. He recounted his experiences with one client in particular, Simon. Oliver had
been involved in supporting Simon through his transition from a local long-stay mental handicap hospital to
his first home in the community. Simon had profound
learning disabilities and limited speech. Oliver's account
indicated a sense of his own futility in 'not changing'
Simon. Perhaps he harboured an implicit belief that the
keyworking relationship should be a vehicle for
'changing clients' and 'making them better':

I don't think in three years we ever got Simon to change
his vocabulary or to use more appropriate behaviours.

Oliver's account seems to reflect many staff's experiences of not seeing changes as a result of their work with
clients, sometimes leading to feelings of their own inadequacy.

Later in the interview we asked Oliver how he thought
Simon had reacted when Oliver had left the residential
home for another job. Oliver indicated a sense of his
own dispensability and possibly a feeling that anyone
can slot into the role of a keyworker:

I don't think he missed me … honestly in all my experi-
ence with working with clients, I don't think any client has

*ever missed me ... the clients might miss the times [spent
with a keyworker], but I mean they might not relate the
times to the person – I don't know. Do you know what I
mean? 'Oh, here's so and so, he does this and he does that,
he baths me here and he baths me there, and I get some
beers in the pub, and we have a laugh', but they might not
relate that to the member of staff – do you know what I
mean?*

These comments also reflect a sense of having invested
energy into a relationship with a client and feeling
uncertain about how much of oneself one should put
into one's work, often getting little in return. Oliver's
perception of his own dispensablity suggests a feeling of
staff being devalued by the system of care, much like the
clients with whom they work.

Nicola offered a different account of her relationship
with a client. She referred to her strong involvement
with Susan and the development of a mutually
dependent relationship. Susan was Nicola's first one-to-
one client and Nicola had started her job at the same
time as Susan moved to the house. She reflected on her
sense of reciprocity and mutual dependency in her relationship with Susan:

*Susan moved to the house with five other people at the
same time – it was a new house. She was very quiet and
found it difficult to relate to anybody, or any of the staff.
She had a history of depression and not talking. And we
struck up quite a good relationship, because I was fairly
quiet and shy at that time anyway ... so it was almost like
a mutual dependency ... We built up a real, like relationship. She mothered me a bit ...*

These accounts of two staff members' perceptions of
the keyworking role represent very different views about
the necessity of emotional detachment versus involve-

ment with clients. Nearly all staff, in describing their role, highlighted the intimate aspects of their work: the personal care of, and proximity to, clients – both emotional and physical – is part and parcel of the job. Many of the staff's accounts indicated a sense of feeling both important and central to the client's world, and not important at all. There were recurring questions about how close keyworkers should get to clients and how dispensable keyworkers are.

The staff's perceptions of their roles as keyworkers fell broadly into four categories: provider, meaning maker, companion and family. These categories overlap with those of the clients' accounts (described in the first part of this chapter), and also correspond quite closely to the classification developed by Clegg et al. (1996). We describe each category below, and then return to the central theme of emotional closeness.

Provider

Many of the staff interviewed commented on the general and expected duties and responsibilities of the keyworker as a 'provider' for clients. The theme of responsibility recurred within the staff's accounts, and was often combined with ideas about general supervision and overall care of residents. In this provider role, the keyworker is often the resident's 'primary carer'.

The accounts from staff suggested two distinct aspects of the provider role. The first related to the 'physical' aspects of looking after clients, involving direct, often intimate care and support. The second aspect encompassed the practical responsibilities of the keyworker – appointments, forms, paperwork and generally a clearly defined support-worker's role, almost 'without getting one's hands dirty'.

The 'physical' aspect of the provider role is described by Karen:

Alan needs a lot of help, a lot of supervision – there were lots of different things that Alan could do, but he could never see a task perhaps fully through – to bathe himself, he might forget to put the plug even in the bath. Then he would come and say, 'There's no water.' There might be another time when the water is too cold because he's forgot to turn the hot on.

Karen's account of supervising and assisting with the physical care of her client, Alan, offers a clear example of the 'provider' role in supporting the resident with activities of daily living. This is a relationship 'where the client's basic needs are met' (Clegg et al., 1996, p. 254). It reflects quite a one-sided relationship, and is possibly the more commonly perceived role of staff in their capacity to support residents to live in the community.

Rob was working with Dan, a man in his mid-twenties. The two men (carer and client) were approximately the same age. Dan was physically disabled and very dependent on Rob as his keyworker for activities of daily living. He could not move his legs, and had mild learning disabilities. Rob's account is striking in its honesty about the 'messy' and undignified elements of keyworking:

I think we did have a very good relationship really. Sometimes it was very hard work – also because I was doing a lot of physical stuff for him, just in my day-to-day job. So sometimes you can see so much of someone that keyworking suffers because of it, do you know what I mean? ... and he was incontinent of both urine and faeces, and I might spend a morning cleaning him up – you would feel quite drained, don't you. So then definitely our keyworking time would go out of the window.

Like many staff, Rob was cleaning and changing an adult who could not care for himself. Such a level of hands-on care is often required with clients who have profound disabilities or who display 'challenging behaviour'. Rob felt that the hands-on physical care of Dan was so time-consuming that it sometimes got in the way of having a more meaningful relationship with Dan. More implicitly, Rob's comments express the pain of experiencing his client as someone without basic dignity and control – something possibly too painful to even mention.

This point was illustrated to us even more forcefully by a conversation one of us had with some staff after our study had ended. Staff teams who are caring for clients with 'challenging behaviours' often have to deal with faecal smearing, which can be seen as a very powerful communication. In discussing this with a group of young and committed staff, it became apparent to us that the staff felt quite overwhelmed by one particular client's behaviours. Reflecting on his personal experiences two weeks into the job, one staff member explained:

We went to the supermarket for the shopping and Abdul was pushing the trolley, he let go for one moment and I took hold of the handle. There was faeces smeared all over the bar. It went all over my hands. I was mortified.

This account describes a filthy and thankless part of the keyworker's job. It is a powerful depiction of the very challenging and often undervalued nature of the work of care staff, which is often skimmed over or forgotten about when considering the roles of staff.

Another keyworker in our study, Tom, succinctly captured the second part of the 'provider' relationship – that of practical responsibility and organisational care:

I would be responsible for Monty's medical appointments, make sure he had regular physiotherapy, that all the dentistry was sorted out, opticians, make sure that his drugs were reviewed properly, due to his epilepsy and stuff like that ... obviously general hygiene, make sure that he was clothed properly, that there was contact with his family. Basically things that I would do for myself that he either couldn't or wouldn't do ...

Similarly, Alex described the practical responsibilities of being a keyworker:

As a keyworker for Frank it was just a case of being responsible for him ... it was all the paperwork linked with Frank. All his care plans and everything were down to me. Anything he needed like having his haircut or something I was responsible. It doesn't mean that I would have to take him, it just means that I would have to sort it out ... He could get quite demanding ... I could be writing a report or something, and he has actually put his face between my face and the paper, just to get my attention and I have just ignored him and carried on ... He saw me as someone who was close to him, but I couldn't be with him all the time.

These descriptions of the keyworker role as focusing on organisational responsibilities suggest a sense of emotional detachment on the part of the keyworker. With the emphasis on making appointments, paperwork and administration, this view of keyworking is perhaps more comfortable for staff: greater emotional involvement may raise some uncomfortable feelings, as is discussed later in this chapter.

Both aspects of the provider role – physical care and practical responsibilities – recurred throughout the staff's accounts of their relationships with clients. This kind of care may be what staff initially expect to do as keyworkers: the provider role is often what is outlined in job descriptions. However, the keyworking relationship is often more complex than simply providing physical

and practical support, as the categories described below
indicate.

Meaning Maker

Engaging with clients and endeavouring to make sense
of their communications was an important part of the
keyworker role described by many staff. As Clegg et al.
(1996) have noted, keyworkers often act as 'meaning
makers', interpreting the feelings and needs that residents may have difficulty expressing directly
themselves. In order to do this, keyworkers need to
spend time with the residents, slowly building up the
relationship and getting to know them well. In essence,
the keyworker strives to understand the person and to
explore what she might want or think, or how she might
feel. This can be especially challenging if the client does
not communicate verbally.

Rob's description of his relationship with Dan reflects
important features of this aspect of keyworking:

> *You know, when someone is feeling something and they
> can't communicate it to you. So I spent quite a lot of time
> with him because he often seemed to have problems – he
> was quite depressed and that, so I would try and find out
> the cause of things. I don't know whether I ever did fully.*

Many staff described their efforts to work with residents towards processing and expressing their feelings:

> *Part of our relationship was about ... just trying to get her
> to express herself for whatever reason.* (Barbara)

> *I was very focused on the practical things [at first] in order
> to hopefully make him feel a bit less anxious about stuff,
> and also just his relationships with everyone else in the
> house, and then a bit later on we concentrated on more*

emotional things like his relationships and his family and trying to enable him to talk about things which he was feeling, which was quite difficult. (Lucy)

Making meaning of clients' communications can be a lengthy process. Sam indicated something about the time that it can take to get to know someone in order to attempt to represent their voice, and how a reciprocal understanding of each other can develop. In his work with Jack, he felt that 'meaning making' eventually operated as a two-way process:

I think that we had a relationship that was built on – I mean in the first instance Jack gave me enormous amounts of grief and I took it I suppose. It ended up with us having an understanding of each other and of the way each other operated, if you like.

Sam went on to explain how the process of making meaning extended to ensuring that other people took the time to engage with and understand the resident:

[My role involved] considering Jack's feelings in what was going on, and making sure that other people were aware of – this is why we are doing this … It was an advocacy role, I think, in a lot of ways.

These accounts of making meaning bear similarities to the clients' accounts of the 'nurturing' role of staff, who make sense of their experiences and allow them to feel emotionally cared for. For clients with limited verbal abilities, it can be difficult to engage in the external world; for staff, it can be difficult and painful to enter into the client's internal life. Perhaps this is one of the most emotionally and intellectually demanding aspects of care work – attempting to make sense of what is happening for someone else.

Companion

Staff's descriptions of the keyworker role often referred to being a 'companion': engaging in joint activities, having common hobbies, or simply enjoying each other's company. Staff described going on excursions with clients, including holidays and shopping trips, and generally going out socially together. Sometimes this aspect of the relationship was described by staff with surprise, as though it was an unexpected bonus for staff to experience pleasure within the relationship. Shared activities or, for some, simply spending quiet time together seemed crucial to the development of a good keyworking relationship:

> We'd go out for dinner, or we'd go to the cinema – just little things like that you know ... we'd go out shopping for clothes together. So the relationship did build up because of the things that we'd done together. (Nia)

Implicit in this aspect of the relationship was a recognition of the individuality of the resident, and an appreciation of her character. Often there was a sense of a reciprocal and mutually enjoyable relationship:

> With me and Monty there was a definite click, just because of musical interests and he loved going to the theatre ... I had a very good relationship with Monty compared to the other clients, but that wasn't because of being a keyworker, that was simply because Monty was a person that I rather liked ... A lot of people saw the disability. I saw the person. (Tom)

> He appreciated my sense of humour. (Oliver)

> Just sitting – having a drink – watching the world go by – chatting with each other and things like that ... I think

there was a respect there – of my space, my feelings – in
the same way as I respected him I suppose. (Sam)

Alice described her relationship with Sally with a sense
of surprise that the time spent together was so enjoyable:

I don't feel a sense of possessiveness with Sally, I wouldn't
allow myself to become possessive. But what I do feel for
her is empathy ... she's good company, she's got something
about her. On a one-to-one when we go out shopping,
she's very lady-like, she's very good company and I really
want to be with her ... I don't know how deep it goes with
Sally, I mean I can only speak for me. When Sally and I
are together sometimes – what she says, it feels really
genuine ... I will miss her.

Family

As a result of working so closely with clients, keyworkers
often felt that they entered into a kind of family role: the
staff–client relationship seemed to replace or mirror
particular family dynamics. This happened in two ways.
Sometimes staff indicated a sense of being a parent to
residents, while in other cases staff felt as if they were the
children being parented by the residents.

In many instances, staff recalled their experiences of
residents responding to them as children would respond
to parents. These accounts suggested a parental transference, with the resident seeking closeness and
protection from the keyworker. As one keyworker,
Karen, put it: *He [the resident] saw me more like a mother*
figure, like he does his older sister.

There was often a sense of familiarity in the
keyworker relationship, with staff feeling bound to
behave as a parent would. Sam described how he
behaved towards his client, Jack, in ways which paral-
leled his behaviour with his own daughter:

> *He [Jack] knew how I would react – in the same way as*
> *there are times when my little girl says to me 'Thanks for*
> *stopping me for doing whatever'* ... *Jack needed the*
> *control aspect of the relationship sometimes.*

In other keyworking relationships, however, staff described feeling like a child in relation to their client. This was especially evident in the accounts of staff who were much younger, with residents being of the same generation as their own parents. In these cases, the keyworker sometimes seemed to be the child that the resident had never had. Nicola described a very significant keyworking relationship with her client, Susan, who was substantially older than Nicola. There seemed to be a very strong attachment between them:

> *It was more like an auntie-type thing. And for her*
> *[Susan], probably somebody that she could mother* ...
> *every time I wasn't well, it would be her that comforted me*
> *and stuff* ... *looked after me.*

Charlotte, a young keyworker in her late twenties, described her relationship with Paul, an older man with mild learning disabilities:

> ... *it felt sort of like talking to someone almost like your*
> *dad at times* ... *He was in his fifties and I was in my late*
> *twenties* ... *so there was that big sort of thing – the protec-*
> *tive thing.*

Charlotte went on to explain that her relationship with Paul was initially quite a struggle, because he had his own interests and did not like spending time with the other residents. Paul had worked in the laundry of a long-stay hospital for many years. He had been institutionalised as a child, because of 'behavioural difficulties'. When Charlotte began to work with Paul he was living in a large community home with seven co-residents. He related more to the staff than to the clients and seemed to feel quite protective over what was predominantly a female staff team. In a sense, he acted as a 'father' not only to Charlotte but to the team:

> *If any of the other residents were verbally abusive you could see Paul get uptight and be sort of protective ... he would stay up later than the staff 'cause he wanted to check that all the windows and doors were locked ... he just wanted to check that everything was OK.*

Other staff described how the residents almost became a replacement for their own family. Living with the residents and becoming immersed in their lives, staff sometimes experienced them as surrogate family members:

> *Really it's like my family. You know I spend more time with the guys here than I do with my family, because my family live away – but deep down you know that the guys aren't your family, and eventually you will have to move on.* (Jenny)

> *I think at the end of the day, it's not just doing your job – it's more. It becomes part of you. My home life and my work life all becomes one thing. Because you spend all your time almost at work – you sleep at work and you are there more than you are at home, and it all ends up a bit of a mix. Everything gets rolled into one – you as a person add your own personality and the people you are around and the clients you are with, it all just ends up as one. You can lose your personality I think – quite easily in residential work.* (Ben)

As Ben's account suggests, residential care is an unusual work setting, where work and home life can merge and where the boundaries between the two can be confusing. For some staff, this setting undoubtedly resonates with the experience of visiting or living with family members. The intimacy of the residential setting perhaps makes it unsurprising that keyworkers are regularly struggling with the concept of intimacy with clients.

How Close should you Get?

How close should the keyworker become to the client? Is it better to keep an emotional distance? And how valued or indispensable is the keyworker to the client? These questions recurred throughout staff's accounts and were often coupled with a sense of guilt about crossing a certain boundary with clients. Nicola mulled over these issues:

I think you can't be distant in this work, because it's their home. And you can't just push someone away, you have to be close ... It's very difficult because you don't know how close to get to people and you think about moving on in a few years time, and should you constantly give that closeness, and then take it away, or should you be quite distant, and be there for everyday things and keep your distance?

Interviewer: Are you saying that you can become over-involved sometimes as a keyworker?

Yes, definitely – especially if you see someone who has come from such a bad background, and you can tell is suffering, and who is not used to ... who you don't think has got anybody there for them. And you sit and listen and try and help them and stuff. I think I just take people's emotions on too much, and I feel too much for them and do like personal things, like sending postcards ... it is very hard because I think I should be more professional [with

*clients] and then I think why shouldn't they have ever
been given that [closeness] in the past?*

Nicola was not at all atypical in her dilemma about
how emotionally involved to get with clients. Her
natural inclination was to have a very personal relationship – and she felt that this was often what clients
needed, given their impoverished social backgrounds.
But she also worried about the consequences – the
emotional overload on herself and the loss the client
might experience when their relationship ended.

In contrast, Tom had very clear ideas about appropriate levels of intimacy in the keyworking relationship.
Tom dipped in and out of care work with adults with
learning disabilities, combining it with a less predictable
career in the theatre. He preferred a subtle 'holding in
mind' attitude to his clients, rather than an overtly close
special keyworking relationship:

*I always think a good keyworker is someone who can do
the job without making it look like they're singling out that
person as their client. I think you should be able to do it
quite subtly ... a good keyworker does it quietly I think.*

Some staff replied to our questions about emotional
closeness in terms of what they thought their clients
understood and expected from the the keyworking
relationship. For example, Pete described his uncertainty about the level of understanding his client, Kevin,
had about their relationship:

*It was difficult to know what Kevin understood by a rela-
tionship. He didn't have, he wouldn't really know what a
friend was. He couldn't really understand emotional and
relationships. So I don't think he would really understand
the kind of link there. But I do know that he would understand that Pete was the person that was with Kevin a lot*

of the time – more so than other members of staff, and it got to the point where I think he could trust me, and if there was a problem he would ask me.

Pete implied that Kevin perceived, and appreciated, the keyworker role as simply that of provider and carer. He believed that Kevin did not expect – or indeed understand – a more personal, or emotional, type of relationship.

It struck us that keyworkers rarely asked clients about their expectations for, or experiences of, the keyworking relationship. Often keyworkers seemed to make assumptions about what they thought the client wanted, and then acted (with the best of intentions) on these assumptions. Our impression was that keyworkers frequently underestimated the importance of their relationships with clients, and that perhaps this was a defence against the conflicting and confusing feelings keyworkers experienced. The idea of being a 'provider' – giving concrete help or providing a 'service' – may be easier for staff to manage psychologically, than being a companion or friend – having a close, emotional relationship. We will return to this issue in Chapter 8.

SUMMARY

There were striking similarities between the accounts given by clients and staff about the role of the keyworker. It was clear that both clients and staff saw the role as multifaceted: the keyworker was seen as someone who offers practical, physical and emotional support to clients, and who often becomes a central part of their lives.

The residents' representations of staff as 'providers' and 'nurturers' very closely matched staff members' accounts of their roles as 'providers' and 'meaning makers'. These roles clearly reflected the dependency of clients on staff – dependency for both practical and emotional care. Both staff and clients also referred to the companionship element of their relationships, and to their appreciation of each other's personality and individual characteristics. There was a sense from both groups of mutual enjoyment and shared understanding, special times and fond and lasting memories of each other.

The accounts of clients and staff alike pointed to the intimacy of the keyworking relationship. For clients, the keyworker was often seen as a close friend and confidant. There was an important sense of feeling 'known' by the keyworker, particularly in the absence of other important relationships in clients' lives. For staff, too, a close relationship with clients often developed. The unusual setting of residential care meant that work and home life sometimes merged for staff: living together, residents and staff experienced each other almost as family members.

Throughout the interviews, many staff returned to a fundamental dilemma, or ambivalence, about the keyworking relationship. They often recognised their importance to clients (and the clients' importance to themselves), but also felt uncomfortable with the closeness of their relationship. They worried about the consequences of becoming close – the emotional overload on themselves and the potential distress of the client when they left. The residents' dependency may have felt all too painful for staff in the face of the reality that this is a group of adults who will never gain full independence. The system of residential care thus raises complex issues and ambiguities for staff; it is therefore not surprising that keyworkers struggled with the issue of how close they should get and what the relationship meant, both for the client and for themselves. We discuss this further in Chapter 9.

CHAPTER 5

How Keyworkers Leave

*It was difficult to talk [with my keyworker about leaving]
... the office was upstairs, and I couldn't climb the stairs
... So it was difficult to be on our own, to be private ... It
was hard for both of us to express at that time ... It would
have had to be on our own. I couldn't have had anybody
around because that would have meant that the privacy
was gone – and I wanted privacy on our own ... We did
have a leaving party, but that was besides the point you
know ... Because you can't take away the feelings inside
... I mean, I take the break-up of my parents. That's
another sad example. I mean it was July 9th, 1968, when
my parents separated and that's going back quite a while.*

This is how Jim described his experience of saying
goodbye to Jean, his favourite keyworker of two years
who had been working in his previous home. He had
enjoyed a very close working relationship with Jean, and
he clearly would have liked to talk with her about their
impending separation. His description points to the
practical constraints – the lack of an accessible, private
space in which to talk – which made this difficult, as well
as the emotional difficulties clients and keyworkers alike
may experience in saying goodbye.

This chapter describes the process of separation, that
is, what staff do and say when their relationship with a
client is coming to an end. Such endings may occur in a
variety of circumstances, for example, when a staff
member is moving on to a new job, going on maternity
leave, or not continuing in their role as keyworker

because of a change in staff roles within the home. The first part of the chapter presents clients' accounts of how keyworkers leave and how the relationship is (or is not) brought to a close. The second part presents staff's accounts. The third, summary section draws together the two sets of accounts.

CLIENTS' ACCOUNTS

Three main themes captured clients' descriptions of how staff departed. These were: 'sudden endings', 'goodbye pleasantries', and 'keeping in touch'.

Sudden Endings

It was very sudden – she just went – like that. (Audrey)

He gone off – and that's it. (Diana)

I said goodbye and she was gone. (Guy)

Two-thirds of the clients we interviewed described an abrupt ending with little or no preparation or chance to say goodbye. Many of the clients were able to comment on their recollections of the absence of preparation. What came through in these accounts was a sense of the suddenness of the change, the not knowing, and the accompanying feelings of confusion, bewilderment and abandonment.

In Eve's case, the sudden ending did not involve an actual departure, but a change in keyworkers within the home. This seems to be quite a common process in group homes, which often have a policy of rotating keyworkers at regular intervals. Several staff in our study explained this as an attempt to prevent client relationships with staff from becoming too intense or close. In other instances, keyworkers change because of staff promotion: for example, a keyworker may take on a management position, relinquishing her responsibilities as a keyworker but remaining in contact with clients. There will also be times (as Eve explains below) when the staff are struggling with being a keyworker to more than one client and the 'responsibility' for a client is handed to a different member of staff:

> *Norah came up to me one day when she was doing a sleep-in and I didn't even realise until she told me that she was going to be my keyworker.... 'cause Mandy couldn't cope with two of us, I mean me and Hilary, so Mandy's only Hilary's keyworker now.... [It felt] a bit embarassing...when she said she couldn't cope with two of us residents.... [She had] too much work on, because of two, because she couldn't cope with two clients.*[1]

Eve reported her discovery of a change in keyworker as almost accidental, and connected with staffing issues. This abrupt process of staff change seemed to impact on her sense of herself: she saw herself almost as a burden to the staff team.

Eve was amongst many of the clients who were able to clearly recall the events surrounding the day they were told of a staff change or departure, perhaps suggesting the traumatic impact of this news. They could often identify the limited time between being told and the keyworker actually leaving. Sally, for example, described her abrupt ending with her keyworker: *She told me she was going the next day. I didn't know – she just stopped working here.*

One could argue that the endings described by residents may have appeared more sudden than they actually were because of the residents' particular needs for lengthy preparation and the provision of repeated

---

1. The full interview with Eve is presented in Appendix C as an example of an interview with a resident.

and clear messages over time (Emerson, 1977). However, their descriptions of unforeseen and sudden endings are consistent with the accounts of many staff (described later in this chapter), who reported either not having said goodbye at all to clients, or who described a 'gradual preparation' – 'gradual' meaning, in some cases, giving only a few days' notice.

Experiences of unanticipated separations from staff will arguably have significant effects on residents. As Zinkin (1994) suggests, 'there is a difference between bringing something to an end and just stopping' (p. 18). According to Wortman and Silver's (1992) model of factors relating to adjustment after loss, the impact on clients will depend largely on whether it can be incorporated into their 'view of the world' and their expectations of events. The suddenness of loss and the conditions in which it occurs can contribute to the shattering of people's 'world view' about the predictability of events. A relationship which ends precipitously, or without time for processing the feelings of loss, will be especially likely to violate assumptions of predictability: people may come to see the world as uncontrollable. Such endings may contribute to a sense of helplessness in clients, an issue we will return to in Chapter 6.

Goodbye Pleasantries

> *Emily took me to the pub and that, and she told me she was going the next day. I got upset, I didn't want her to go. She said, 'I'll give you something to think of me.' She gave me some soap – it's in there [pointing to the cupboard in her room].* (Sally)

Like Sally, several clients we interviewed described how their experience of saying goodbye to their keyworker had been marked by pleasant rituals or 'happy events' in the home. There were reports of meals out and parties.

In some cases, clients had received gifts from staff, as
Sally had done. In other cases, clients themselves were
encouraged to provide the leaving presents. Audrey
described her plans for saying goodbye to her current
keyworker, Julia: *I'll buy some flowers for Julia, some
chocolates. Will miss her.*

However, some clients seemed to question how far
these events could assist with the pain and inevitability
of separation. Jim reflected:

> *We did have a leaving party, but that was besides the
> point you know ... Well I know it's not a question of
> shaking the hand and saying goodbye. It's something more
> emotional than that I think.*

Clients such as Jim seemed to have some insight into the
reality of saying goodbye, which cannot be masked by
'quick fixes'. Whilst clients often reported a 'happy' end
to the keyworking relationship, clearly this did not
prevent or undo the pain of separation.

Molly's account of the recent departure of her
keyworker, Louise, indicates some of her very painful
feelings about the separation. Molly was 35 and had
spent many years in a convent. When she was in her late
twenties she was moved to a large staffed residential
home. Little was known about her childhood and young
adulthood. She described staff and managers as
'rescuers' who came to the convent and took her away
and moved her into her community home. Molly spent
most of her time in our interview describing her close
relationship with Louise, and how Louise had left the
previous week because she was going to have a baby:

> *Louise was due to go on maternity leave, she's going to go
> on maternity leave and her stomach got bigger and bigger,
> and suddenly she couldn't do any more and she had to
> leave last Monday, and she took us out. We had a meal*

with her – a Chinese meal – we had a last meal with her
... we loved her and we kissed her. We all felt very upset
about it. All of us, Greg and me and Diana [co-residents].
We all felt very upset, she's left us.

Molly not only seemed anxious about how she would
be looked after in the future, but her feelings about losing
Louise as her keyworker also may have been connected
with issues of fertility and her own missed opportunities
for relationships and procreation. Thus, Louise's departure may have generated complex feelings of loss for
Molly, yet there seems to have been nowhere for her to
take those feelings. A meal out and a pleasant goodbye
clearly could not begin to address these feelings.

These 'goodbye pleasantries' raise questions about the
effects on residents (and staff) of not directly addressing
the painful aspects of separation. Pleasant rituals such as
meals out and parties may be important for marking the
end of important relationships, for both staff and clients.
However, such rituals may also mask painful feelings on
both sides, and serve as a convenient way to avoid
confronting these feelings. A central issue, which we will
return to in later chapters, is how clients can be assisted
to face the painful reality of endings, a process which can
clearly take a great deal of time. Until that reality has
been acknowledged and accepted, it may not be possible
for a period of healthy mourning to begin.

Keeping in Touch

It would be nice to see them [previous keyworkers] again,
just to say hello and how are you and to see briefly what
they're doing. (Jim)

When we asked clients to describe how their relationships with previous keyworkers had been brought to a
close, many brought up their (often unfulfilled) desire to

keep in touch with keyworkers after they had left. For some, like Jim, brief contact was all that was wanted: a chance to say hello and to tell each other about developments in their lives since the keyworker's departure.

Those who did refer to having contact with keyworkers again seemed satisfied with even the most minimal gesture: *She sends me postcards. I like that* (Catherine). One resident looked happy and excited as she talked about meeting up briefly by chance with her previous keyworker: *Then I saw her again, twice in church, and she looked me up and down, and she wanted to know where I lived and I told her* (Lilly). There was a certainty in many of the clients' accounts that the opportunity to see the staff again was to be taken: *Most people who have left I have seen again. I think that's a good thing* (Guy).

Some residents reported their failed attempts at keeping in touch with keyworkers. Catherine explained: *I've got her [previous keyworker's] telephone number.* (Interviewer: Do you ever telephone her?) *No, because there's no answer – I do try sometimes.*

Sometimes the residents described their longing to see staff again, but they seemed to recognise their lack of control over contact in reality, as Sally lamented: *Can't get in touch, don't know where she is.*

There was also a sense of clients having to rely on other staff to support this contact: *I can't go on my own [to visit previous keyworker] – I would if I could* (Jim).

These accounts from clients point not only to their desire for keeping in touch, but to their lack of control over seeing keyworkers again. A painful reminder of the imbalance in the keyworking relationship emerges in their realisations that it may be beyond their control to maintain contact with staff who were important to them. Staff are usually able to locate residents with whom they have previously worked, but residents often have no knowledge of the whereabouts of staff after their departure.

As Rosenberg (1990) has pointed out, staff take the lead in establishing the structure of the relationship – deciding what will be done, when it will be done and how it will be done. It is the keyworker who also decides when, and how, to move away from the relationship. This imbalance may contribute to feelings of powerlessness and failure in the client.

STAFF ACCOUNTS

The client asked me, looking very worried and upset and said, 'You're not leaving are you?' And somebody dived in and said, 'No, he's going on holiday', which I felt quite awful about. I could see why they said it though. So as far as I know, they were told I was going on holiday, just to tide the situation over for a few days, because it was a really dangerous situation in that home. I said bye bye to him, but I never said I'm not coming back. (Alex)

Alex was a young keyworker who had worked with Frank for only a few months, but had developed a very good relationship with him in a relatively short time. Alex was working in a large residential home with ten clients. The staff–client ratio was very low and the environment was reportedly extremely stressful. Alex was afraid of telling the clients that he was leaving because things were already so bad in the home. However, he also suggested that someone else had 'dived in' to offer an explanation to clients, thereby denying everyone the opportunity to say goodbye. There was something quite powerless about Alex's account of his experience as a member of staff at the home. Perhaps that powerlessness reflected the residents' daily experiences of things happening to them that were beyond their control.

Goodbyes are notoriously difficult to tolerate and to manage. Each of us has our own ways of avoiding or marking what is often a painful severing of a relationship or bond. Our study focused on the process of separation between residential staff and clients and their opportunities (or lack of opportunities) for saying goodbye. The staff's recollections of separations from clients touched on their actual preparation plans; saying goodbye (or not) to residents; marking the occasion with parties and presents; and questions about whether or not to keep in touch. There was a recurring theme of lack of support and supervision structures for staff, which seemed to have a great impact on the process of saying goodbye. This issue of support will be explored in a separate section later in this chapter.

Abrupt Departures

Over one-third of the staff we interviewed reported not having said goodbye to their clients prior to their separation. They recalled various reasons for their abrupt departures: some said there were external factors beyond their control, while others said they were uncertain about the correct approach to take.

A number of staff described their own grievances with management, and their decisions to leave suddenly and without warning. Oliver had become a manager himself of a different group home at the time of our interview, but he was still angry about his own past experiences of residential care work and the difficult interface with his previous manager. This experience had led him to make an abrupt departure with no opportunity for goodbyes:

I actually walked out [laughs] – personal reasons with the unit. I took a grievance up against the manager and I just walked out ... and I mean I did go back [four months later] – everyone always says, 'I'll come back and see you' – very, very few people do so. I went back a few times and took him [Simon, his previous client] out, but then I was told that if I actually wanted to see Simon, I'd have to tell them in advance. And I was going to take that up with my union, because that's not what residential work is about – you should be able to phone up and say, 'I'm coming now' ...

Clearly in this case, Simon was a casualty of something wider than his relationship with his keyworker. Oliver was obviously angry with the systems within which he was working and this anger intruded into his sense of what might have been best for his client at the time.

Barbara had worked in residential care for six years at the time of our interview. She spent a great deal of time describing her relationship with a client called Liz, with whom she had developed a very good relationship. Barbara described a long preparation for saying goodbye to Liz, because she had learned from some very difficult previous experiences in group homes that preparation was important for clients. In her first job as a keyworker, she was denied the opportunity to say goodbye to her clients because of an incident where one of the other residents in the home had become quite aggressive towards Barbara:

The day I left [my first job], the people I was working with didn't know that was my last shift, and none of the residents knew that was my last shift. But the understanding was that the care manager was going to tell everybody.

Interviewer: So were you not allowed to say anything to the clients?

No, she [the care manager] wanted to talk to the clients prior to that and so on the last evening, I was like. 'Thanks for working with me and all that.' And they [other staff] were like. 'Where are you going?' And I was like, 'I finish at 8.00 tonight you know.' I felt gutted.

Barbara later alluded to the impact of leaving suddenly on her own personal and professional sense of feeling valued:

> *It affects the way you react with people. I felt very under-valued, definitely, and I wish I had spent time with clients, because I was very concerned – if they could treat me like that, then what about the clients – how would they continue to treat them? I think you can communicate to them events and leaving. So I found it very hard to take. And I think professionally as well. It's like you're nobody. Well not necessarily that you're nobody, but no one's … I mean I had done quite a lot of personal work with one client in particular, and a month after I left he died, and I didn't even have a chance to say goodbye professionally, and personally for him to know that every-thing we talked about quite personally was maintained and not gossiped about. The way I would like to finish something is by spending a lot of time with someone personally.*

Barbara reflected on her sense of unimportance and insignificance in the face of her enforced abrupt depar-ture from the home. In this instance it was the keyworker who had no control over the decision to move away. Perhaps Barbara's sense of being 'nobody' or 'no one's' mirrors the residents' uncertainties and insecur-ities when someone close to them leaves suddenly and without preparation. For many clients there may be a feeling of not being worthy of an explanation or pre-paration for saying their goodbyes to staff.

Barbara also raised an important issue about trust and security in the keyworking relationship. It may not be easy for clients to articulate the importance of devel-oping a relationship in which personal experiences and feelings can be disclosed. However, it is perhaps unsur-prising that some residents find it difficult to continue to trust new staff – because inevitably many staff will leave, taking with them a part of the residents' lives.

Like Barbara, Jenny was another keyworker who had been involved in a difficult incident with a particular resident, and had been encouraged by management to leave immediately, for her own safety. Jenny told us: *I wasn't even allowed to say goodbye – even to the other clients.* Jenny felt powerless in this situation; she wanted to mark the end of her relationship with residents but was prevented from doing so.

Some staff explained that they themselves had not realised that they would not be seeing residents again. Debbie, for example, was given the opportunity to transfer to a smaller residential unit from a large long-stay ward for adults with learning disabilities. She was keen to leave, but she was also asked to go on training immediately; consequently she was denied the opportunity for 'planned goodbyes' to clients who had been in her care for a long period of time:

> *When I left I didn't realise it was my last shift working there ... So it was a shock to go home and realise that I wouldn't be going back there – that the next day I would be doing something else.*

> Interviewer: Can you remember how you felt afterwards?

> *It felt sad knowing that I would not be back and I hadn't really had a chance to spend time with them ... To think that we never had the chance to say goodbye. One day we were there and the next we were gone.*

A few staff we spoke to attributed their not having said goodbye to their uncertainty about the correct course of action to be taken. Lucy described the absence of direction or guidelines from management:

I was having quite a dilemma about how long before I was actually leaving that I should be letting people know. I mean there were no guidelines or anything within the organisation ... it was very much left down to me. I had to create a kind of wind-down for myself.

Lucy had handed in her resignation because she was planning to pursue a social work training course. She had worked with her client, Oscar, for 18 months and they had enjoyed a close working relationship. Lucy wanted to think with Oscar about their goodbye, but she was not confident in her own judgement of the situation and how much to prepare her client. Lucy was also not sure about who would replace her, or how long it would take until Oscar had a new keyworker, and that added to her own uncertainty about the most appropriate course of action:

I think Oscar was focused on who was going to come in to replace me rather than my leaving ... and I suppose I felt a bit torn between meeting those needs, and also I didn't know who was going to be coming in to replace me, who was going to be his new keyworker, whether it was going to be a man or a woman, good or bad, worse than me or better than me – or whether that was important.

Lucy also wondered whether *not* planning and focusing on the goodbye might be in the best interests of her client:

I tried not to deal with the end. Because I was leaving, it wasn't for me at that point to give him messages he couldn't handle. He was happier to avoid that side of things.

In contrast to Lucy, some staff seemed to be quite clear about what the best course of goodbye preparation might be – especially because they had noticed situations where clients had been shocked and distressed in the absence of preparation for separations from staff. Alice described how her current client, Sally, had been informed that her previous keyworker was leaving. Alice had been able to witness what was actually said because she was already working in Sally's residential home at the time. She felt that the process of saying goodbye had been quite clumsily handled by Emily, Sally's previous keyworker. Emily had told Sally in the kitchen, whilst a few of the other residents and Alice were preparing the evening meal:

> *Emily said, 'Sally, guess what? – I won't be your keyworker any more, Alice will.' Sally screamed out – and I mean screamed out, as though someone had hit her from behind. It was totally unexpected ...*

Alice went on to say how she would have liked Sally to have been prepared:

> *I think a period of meetings – all three of us – would have been better. Just sitting together and talking about things and what was going on and how we could work together. Gradual withdrawal, gradual integration would have been a better way than just in the kitchen – out of nowhere – throwing that like lightning on her.*

As a result of observing this absence of a planned goodbye, Alice had developed quite clear ideas about what might be a 'good goodbye'. This leads to a consideration below of staff who reported planned endings and proper goodbyes to clients.

Planned Endings

The staff in our study had a variety of ideas about what constituted 'planned endings' or 'good goodbyes'. Some

staff felt that a few days' notice was sufficient preparation time for residents, and others were aware that their
clients needed a lot longer than a few days to integrate
the fact that they were saying goodbye to staff and that,
in many cases, they would not be seeing their
keyworkers again.

Pete explained that he had prepared his client,
Kevin, for their goodbye for about a week. He had been
Kevin's keyworker for two years and in that time the
two of them had formed a strong bond. Kevin was 54
years old and had spent his life in institutional and residential care; he had a label of autism and had very
limited verbal communication. Pete told us about the
type of preparation he and the other staff thought Kevin
had needed:

> *We had to build up for it. If he needed a haircut, you had
> to give him a day's notice, and keep reminding him. So
> we decided it would be best if we built it up over a period
> of about a week – to get used to the idea, then he would be
> fine with it. But if you sprung anything on him, like
> 'You're going to have a haircut now', then he would go
> ballistic. So we decided a week because if we told him
> sooner than that – say a month – you would get nothing
> more than 'When's Pete going? When's Pete leaving?'
> And you could tell him one hundred times and he would
> still keep asking.*

Pete described the final goodbye on his day of departure:

> *I was excited that I was leaving, so I kept talking about it
> anyway, but it didn't register [on Kevin] from day to day
> and when I said goodbye for the last time it didn't register
> either. He looked at me, but only as he did when he said
> goodbye every day, so I don't know. Maybe he was
> expecting me back the following morning – I don't know.*

Gill had a very different idea about what constituted adequate preparation. She felt that a longer period of time was necessary for her client to adjust to the loss:

> *Well, I actually started telling Margaret about two months before I left, gradually told her. When I first told her she totally ignored me, turned her head the other way, didn't want to understand, didn't want to know really. Apparently this had been her reaction with other people she had become attached to ... She would ignore it, turn her head, didn't want to know, changed the subject, stopped talking ... And when you started talking about this she would start doing the repetitive speech, switching off, she would totally switch off. So it had to be a long gradual process of telling her that you were actually leaving.*

Gill's experience of saying goodbye reflected her understanding that Margaret needed a long period of time to integrate what was happening. Margaret seemed to regress and become more disabled when hearing the sad news, which indicated to Gill something about needing to persevere, and gently and constantly remind Margaret that the two of them would be parted soon. Gill had the insight and understanding of Margaret to know that she needed time to understand what was happening and to integrate that information and remember.

It can be difficult for staff to determine what clients need (or want) in terms of preparation for staff departures. Different clients may need different types or amounts of preparation, depending on various factors. Some will need an extensive amount of predictability or control over their environment. They may require continual and repeated preparation for change over a long period of time. There may be clients who do not communicate verbally and will require planning and preparation through other non-verbal methods. There will also be clients who do not have other significant relationships in their lives and who will depend more strongly on the permanence of the keyworking relationship, therefore requiring a greater amount of preparation for their loss.

Charlotte was another keyworker who felt that the residents she worked with needed time to process and express their emotions about her departure. Charlotte had worked with Max for two years and explained that it had taken a long time to build up their relationship. She described how she told Max and the other residents about her plans to leave:

> *I gave a month's notice and I think I told the residents quite soon after I gave my month's notice. I think we discussed it in the staff meeting first and then I just sat down individually with people and told people ... I sat down with people one by one and told them that I had got this job and how I was moving back sort of around my family. And that it was a promotion from a support worker to a deputy manager ... I just talked to Max about the reasons as to why it was actually happening. And then it was really – I think it was, he was kind of accepting it, not really showing much emotion at first and then the emotion came out a little bit.*

Charlotte described Max as a very able and insightful young person. He was clearly struck by the news of her planned departure, but needed time to process his feelings before he could make sense of them or express them in any way. Charlotte seemed to be in touch with the fact that Max did need time, and she noticed his gradual moves towards acceptance.

Barbara also indicated her thoughtfulness and careful strategies for supporting her client, Liz, through the process of separation. Barbara's past experiences of leaving clients suddenly and without warning had left her feeling devalued and worried about the clients. She

had developed quite clear ideas about what residents
need and deserve when staff leave:

> *Being quite honest with them ... helping them work through
> their own feelings about that, and helping them to share
> that, and tell people, 'I'm really naffed off.' And for the last
> few weeks we sort of planned things like 'goodbye sessions'.*

Finally, some staff took additional steps to hand over
their role as keyworker in a way that would ensure continuity. Maria told us:

> *I did shifts with the new keyworker for three months before
> he became keyworker, so he would get to know the client
> before he keyworked him and stuff.*

For Maria, part of the process of preparation for saying
goodbye was about allowing her client to become accustomed to someone new. She described a careful process
of transition. However, many staff and clients were
forced to tolerate the uncertainty of not knowing who
would replace a departing keyworker: staff and clients
alike often had to tolerate the fact that there would be a
void in the system of care and support.

Goodbye Pleasantries

> *There's always an event for the person who leaves,
> whether we go out for a meal or a party or stuff. It has
> always ended on happy terms. There's never just a
> goodbye at the end of a shift. There's always a happy
> ending. I think people rely on having a nice memory and
> a happy memory.* (Maria)

The importance of marking the end of the keyworking
relationship was expressed by many of the staff.
However, the nature of these endings was sometimes

difficult to discern. The majority of staff described their attempts to create a 'happy ending'. This kind of marker mirrors the residents' accounts of meals out, parties and visits to the pub – various attempts by the staff to ease the painful transition.

> *I left it two weeks. I had to build myself up to it, and I thought, 'It's difficult for a month for her [the client], thinking, 'When's she going? She said she's going.' So I thought I'd leave it two weeks and in that two weeks there were lots of parties and things like that, so it was easier for her to focus on that two weeks than the months.* (Nicola)

Nicola's account reflects something of her own pain about saying goodbye to her client, which may have been easier to manage through parties and happier distractions. Goodbye parties are a common and often helpful marker of the end of a relationship. However, it was not always easy for staff or clients to find a space for the expression of more difficult feelings about separation. For some staff, a pleasant goodbye was considered sufficient for marking the end of their relationship with a client:

> *There was general chat about me leaving. We had the party, which gave people a chance to say goodbye, and I took him [the client] out. I don't think there would have been anything in addition that I would have done.* (Nia)

However, a few staff described the importance of also recognising the painfulness of saying goodbye. For example, Barbara felt it was important to organise structured times for 'goodbye sessions' where her client could have the opportunity to talk about some of her feelings about saying goodbye and they could think together about what would happen in the future and how things would be in the home:

I think when I was working with Liz at the end it was acknowledged that not everything was going to be of a social content, you know make it all happy, because that would be pointless.

Goodbye pleasantries clearly have their place, but can also be a way of masking or easing the more painful aspects of separation. This may present a dilemma for staff who are wanting to do the best for their clients. Organising parties and ensuring 'happy endings' may be motivated by the staff's desire (conscious or unconscious) to protect their clients, as well as themselves, from the emotional pain of separation. It can be difficult to disentangle the needs of staff and clients when the needs of one part of the keyworking dyad are so often a reflection of the other.

Keeping in Touch

Our questions about keeping in touch at the end of the keyworking relationship led the staff to offer a range of opinions about the merits and drawbacks of promising future contact with residents. The issue of whether to continue seeing former clients links in part to the question of boundaries and emotional over-involvement with clients, which was raised in Chapter 4. Whether or not to keep in touch was one of the main dilemmas referred to by staff, especially in relation to protecting themselves and their clients, and thinking about what can be realistically offered within the staff–client relationship.

I didn't want to have her phone me up at home or anything like that, as far as I'm concerned that's work ... but I'm not prepared to commit myself to her, knowing that I couldn't do it regularly and I don't think she would have benefited from that ... It had to be very clear-cut with Liz ... I said, 'If I'm around I'll call in, but I can't say when', and occasionally I would phone up, but I didn't feel obliged that I had to do it. I felt that I had given for three and a half years as much as I could. (Barbara)

Barbara was one of many staff who were clear about wishing to make a clean break from residents. She identified a need for clarity and boundaries at the end of the keyworking relationship, partly because she felt emotionally drained after several years of working closely with her client. She was also clear about not wanting to give false hopes of future contact. Occasionally staff did promise to keep in touch – although they knew future contact was unlikely – in order to soften the blow of separation. However, false promises, while well-intentioned, are likely to lead to even more disappointment than a clean break.

Maria indicated something about her sense that the ending had to be very final for her own sake:

I had to tell him I was leaving, and that would be it, because obviously for me I didn't want any other contact.

Other staff clearly wanted to avoid confronting a potentially painful reunion:

Probably part of the reason that I haven't gone back, as well as the aggro with the staff, is the fact that I don't really want to know whether or not it had a negative effect [on the client] – me going. (Sam)

Some staff, after leaving their post, were keen to develop new forms of relationships with their former clients. These were described in terms of friendships as well as advocacy roles. These staff seemed to manage to preserve the relationship, but in a different capacity:

It's nicer now, because I know I'm not his keyworker, I don't have to worry about all the rubbish, you know, all the paperwork and documentation. I can just treat him like a friend – it's a lot more relaxed. (Debbie)

A few staff recognised their own need to maintain their relationships with residents. Nicola had left her job as Susan's keyworker to go travelling for two years. She described her desire to keep in contact:

I rang [Susan] regularly, and I was attached as probably she was ...

Interviewer: When you did telephone her and keep in touch, do you think it was for her benefit or for yours or for both of you?

I think it was for both really, because I felt, 'Oh gosh, I'm going off to a strange country.' I was so shy and so, you know, quiet – and I didn't even like going shopping on my own, let alone going to strange countries. And I think part of it was to let Susan know through the process what I was doing and where I was going, so she knew that I wouldn't forget her.

Nicola was obviously anxious about her own new-found independence, as well as leaving Susan behind. Again, for the keyworker in this instance, there seemed to be a mirroring of the client's pain and need for ongoing contact. In many of the accounts given by staff, it was difficult to distinguish the clients' needs from those of the staff.

Nia explained that she continued to visit her old workplace regularly, because she missed her old job and all of the residents: *I pop in on my day off*. However, for Nia, the situation was quite complicated because she also continued to see her previous clients at the local day centre. She had left her former job for a promotion to the post of manager of another home, and her new clients attended the same centre as her old clients. She explained that when she went to collect her new clients, one of her previous clients, Scott, would pick up his coat and want to go home with her:

> *I would pick up our clients to bring them home. He [Scott] would automatically pick up his coat and take his bag and want to come with me, and he would follow me to the car to come with me. And I would be, like, 'No, you're not coming with me', and it would almost be like fighting with him.*

Interestingly, Scott's desire to go back to a familiar relationship was mirrored by Nia, who explained that sometimes she would drive and find herself in the road where her previous workplace was, without consciously planning or even noticing her journey. Nia seemed to share Scott's wish for them to be reunited:

> *It made it a lot harder because when I went to the day centre he would follow me saying, 'I want to go home with you.' And I would be thinking, 'And I want to come home with you too.'*

Nia's account suggests that the process of seeing former clients can be painful for staff: it can be a constant reminder of relationships that have ended or have taken a different form. Similarly, it is possible that some clients may find the experience of seeing their old keyworkers very painful, and a 'clean break' may be easier for some.

Some staff expressed their wish to see residents again, but felt that this was not encouraged by the units in which they had worked:

I think that ... many organisations make it hard for you to go back. Although they [the residents] are adults with adult rights and everything else, they are still very protected by people who have responsibility for them. (Sam)

I kept thinking about her [Margaret], and also being very tempted to sort of visit. If you drove near the home, you'd feel like knocking and saying, 'Can I go in and visit Margaret?' But I was told that it was a good idea to let her have a cooling-off period, of six weeks to two months. But it was very tempting to ring up and say, 'Is it all right to go in and visit Margaret?' (Gill)

Perhaps in some cases there were new staff employed to work with the residents who felt threatened by previous staff, especially when they were not feeling well-supported or valued within their own roles.

A few staff indicated their intention to keep in touch with former clients, but struggled to find the time or take the initiative, leading to feelings of guilt and shame. Oliver expressed this in relation to Simon, a client with whom he had previously worked very closely:

I got feeling very guilty that I didn't take him [Simon] out. I took him out twice, you know, but I promised I'd take him out regularly, but even now I haven't and I still feel guilty when I see him ... I feel guilty about all the clients I have ever worked with, because I know it's a standard thing. Even here [present workplace] we have staff who say, 'I'll come back and see you.' The trouble with Simon was that he is a very special person beyond the call of duty ...

Oliver explained that it was painful when he did see Simon again. He noticed that Simon's skills had deteriorated since Oliver had left and Simon was in someone else's care. He found it upsetting to notice those changes in Simon:

> *I feel so sad, because you put a lot of effort in trying to develop somebody – help someone to develop themselves. You know, when you see things disappear you feel ... I mean when I walk in and see Simon all hunched up – I mean it was 18 months and I finally got him to sit in a chair with his arms up instead of holding them ...*

The diversity of staff responses to questions about keeping in touch with former clients may reflect some of the ambivalence about what is best for whom. There may be situations when staff want to see clients again, but are fearful of what changes they might notice – whether the clients have deteriorated in someone else's care. There may be a fantasy for some staff (as Oliver hints at) of making things better for clients in a long-term sense: almost eliminating the learning disability completely, by offering long-term care and support. This fantasy may arise in response to some of the more difficult feelings relating to caring for someone in the knowledge that they will never be 'cured'.

Staff Support and Supervision

Lack of support was a recurring theme in the staff's reflections on ending their relationships with clients and leaving their places of work. Mostly, the staff reported not being helped at all in thinking about the process of saying goodbye. This lack of support was evident in the daily work of the keyworker and in the low self-worth attached to their perceptions of their own roles. Perhaps there is something wider about how devalued the role of the keyworker is in a more general sense. It is as though the staff are not valued, like the clients in their care. This lack of value attached to the role of the keyworker may be reflected by the staff's not even being able to think about supervision and support in some settings.

In response to our specific questions about support at the time of leaving, some staff reported being made to feel guilty about leaving, and being pressurised by their managers to stay:

What support? Constant wanting me to change my mind before I left ... Making me feel guilty ... I think they also said, 'You can't leave now when people are so attached to you.' (Nicola)

Others referred to minimal general supervision in their roles as keyworkers, which impacted also on the process of leaving their posts. There was an awareness that this lack of personal emotional support would have affected their relationships with residents:

I didn't have any [support]. None at all. I didn't get any in relation to ending relationships or finishing relationships with key clients – things like that. I don't think I had had supervision for six months by the time I left ... but the support for me would have carried down to the residents, because I was supporting them. (Rob)

This lack of support often led to a sense of isolation in staff, who felt misunderstood, with little opportunity for processing their own feelings about leaving:

The only person who really gave me any support was my partner, but it was hard for him because he doesn't understand – he couldn't understand how hard it was for me to leave these people who I've worked with, day in and day out for two and a half years. (Nia)

Sam described his own abrupt departure from a previous job. He had left from the position of acting

manager. He was aware of the pitfalls of his own organisation and yet he felt powerless in the face of more
entrenched and long-standing staffing difficulties:

> *We had a staff team of 11 and we sat down and went
> through the rotas one day, just as I took over as manager
> – so about three years into it. And we had something like
> 78 members of staff in three years ... I think that one of
> the greatest failings of the community care system is the
> staff turnover. I mean in the first two years of that organ-
> isation we had over 300 per cent turnover of staff within
> two years.*

Sam later referred to his experience of saying goodbye
to his client, Jack:

> *It [saying goodbye] didn't really happen – I mean I let
> people know that I would be going and we had a leaving
> party and it was a question of me just going down to the
> Chinese, really – I mean the background was, I was acting
> as manager and we had a team of eight staff and five left
> at the same time as me and we were running on agency
> [staff].*

Sam's account is a sad relection of what happens in
many residential homes in the face of severe staffing
shortages. It can be difficult for staff to find the space to
think about the emotional needs of clients in the context
of heavy work demands. Perhaps the lack of support and
supervision for staff leaving posts underlies the messi-
ness of the work and the demands of caring for adults
with learning disabilities with limited resources and little
reward.

This underlying theme of lack of support and supervision for staff seems to recur in many settings within
the system of care in the community. In our current
clinical work with a residential care-staff team for adults

with learning disabilities, we are attempting to implement guidelines for staff in managing the difficult behaviours of one particular client. In response to our questions about support and supervision, some staff reported that they had not received individual or group supervision in over 18 months. More striking was the fact that they did not even question this absence of support and had almost forgotten how to request it from their manager.

SUMMARY

These accounts of residents' and staff's experiences of separation highlight the sudden and abrupt departures of many keyworkers. For clients, there was a sense of the unexpected nature of those partings leading to shock, confusion and bewilderment. The staff also reported either not having said goodbye at all to clients, or a 'gradual process of preparation', with varying ideas about what constituted gradual, including (in some cases) only a few days' notice.

The suddenness of partings at the end of staff–client relationships, and the residents' experiences of lack of control over that process, links with questions about keeping in touch. The residents in our study seemed satisfied with even the briefest contact with staff after they left. However, a painful reminder of the power imbalance in the keyworking relationship emerged in their realisations that it was usually not their choice and it was not in their control to maintain or renew contact with staff if they had wanted to. The staff were able to locate the clients if they chose to do so, but the residents mostly had no knowledge of the whereabouts of staff after their departure. For staff, there was an uncertainty about maintaining contact with residents – which seemed to parallel their uncertainty about emotional closeness versus professional distance in the keyworking relationship (see Chapter 4). The staff seemed uncertain about what was the most helpful for clients, and they were sometimes drawn to go back, but aware of the pain of holding on to what had been lost.

Both residents and staff reported that the endings of their relationships were often marked by pleasant rituals or goodbye parties. Sometimes these pleasantries seemed to be a way of easing, or avoiding, the painfulness of separation. However, as some residents indicated, such pleasantries clearly did not lessen their emotional distress or offer any solace. In some instances, the clients seemed more willing than the staff to address the impact of parting and to tolerate the pain of saying goodbye. Of course, we are not suggesting that goodbye parties and meals out are inappropriate events when staff leave: it is natural to have a party for someone who is leaving. However, the work setting for the keyworker is home for the client – and for the clients, staff departures represent more than someone simply leaving a job. Goodbye parties are one part of saying goodbye, but they cannot replace the opportunities clients need for expressing the painful feelings aroused by endings.

Perhaps it was too overwhelming for some of the staff to think carefully about what the clients needed or wanted from them. What is striking is that the unsatisfactory nature of many of the endings reported led to feelings of hopelessness and futility on both sides. Ironically, in some instances, the clients had taken responsibility for understanding the needs of staff – that they had families of their own, or that they wanted to travel. It is possible that these clients were offering 'socially desirable responses' (Barrett and Jones, 1996). Perhaps the clients did not always feel able to express their true feelings or knowledge, but rather they felt able to express what they believed was wanted of them. However, it is also possible that the clients – who had a lot of experience of staff departures – were sometimes more in touch with the needs of staff than the staff were with those of the clients.

Despite the difficulties encountered in the process of leaving, some keyworkers seemed to manage well-planned endings with their clients. These keyworkers were thoughtful about residents' needs, allowing them time to understand and assimilate the prospect of change. The clients we interviewed did not tell us about such planned endings, possibly because the unplanned and unexpected endings were more salient. Also, repeated experiences of loss – often without preparation – may have diminished the impact of preparation when it did occur.

CHAPTER 6

Feelings After Leaving: Clients' Stories

Sue said goodbye to me and I was sad but I didn't cry, because sometimes people who cry, the social worker might say very firmly 'Don't be so silly.' You get people like that ... The only thing I cried at was when I had to say goodbye to my mother when she died. She had cancer ... [When] my mum died I said goodbye in a very good way, but I did cry then ... [When staff leave] it's not like they die, it's just that I don't think they'll ever come back.

This was Bill's story about saying goodbye to his keyworker, Sue. Bill was a 44-year-old man, with mild to moderate learning disabilities and mobility problems. He looked older than his 44 years and was dressed in a suit which was crumpled and too small for him. He seemed to be holding tightly to his personal dignity.

Bill had been living in a small shared home in the community for four years. He kept in touch with his father, who visited once every fortnight to take him to the pub. He talked proudly about his sister and brother-in-law, showing us a picture of their wedding day, and he explained: *I was in [the hospital] all locked up when they were getting married, because I ran muck – you know – got very violent, and I didn't go.*

Bill provided a clear and painful account of his life before he had moved to his present home:

I was living at [a local community home] and before that I was living at [the hospital] and it was for twelve years I was at a boarding school and at the end of my tether. At the end of my years of being there – twelve years – I got home, and I lived at home for about one month and I got about 25 pence a week for my pocket money. And then I went to another hospital, and then I lived there and then to [the first hospital] and after that I came to [a local community home], and then I came here.

Bill reflected on some of the moves and changes he had experienced over the past years. He described the various keyworkers in his life, and their personalities seemed to merge in his mind. He was still able to name many of the staff and managers, and he located them in the different homes and hospitals where he had spent his years. He described his relationship with Sue more fully. Sue was obviously a very special keyworker to Bill, and the only one who had maintained contact with him after leaving. Sue and Bill had worked together for five years.

Bill's account was typical of many of the clients' stories about the impact of their separation from staff. Each of the clients we interviewed indicated some of their feelings about their experiences of saying goodbye; their fears about losing keyworkers in the future; their means for expressing more painful feelings; and their perspectives on both other residents and staff who have been affected by this process. These accounts fell broadly within the following themes: loss and grief, helplessness, and acceptance and acquiescence.

Loss and grief

Bill's moving account of saying goodbye to his keyworker led him to spontaneously reflect on his mother's death. In fact many of the clients in our study seemed to automatically make a link between losing a keyworker and their experiences of loss through bereavement.

At the beginning of our study, we attended a residents' meeting in a large staffed house. As we were explaining the purpose of our study, one client shouted out: *Should we talk about people dying too?* This comment encouraged other residents to start recounting their experiences of family and friends dying, and they prompted each other to let us know about experiences of bereavement.

During a telephone conversation to organise a time for the interview, one client asked: *Will I be talking about funerals?* This almost automatic association with death was also apparent in the content of many of the clients' interviews. When asked about his experiences of losing keyworkers, Guy explained: *It makes me feel like I'm never going to see them again. It gives me that feeling.* There was a clear sense of clients' connecting their experiences of saying goodbye to staff with bereavements of family or friends. Catherine said in despair as she was describing her keyworker's departure: *It made me think of my friend dying.*

Catherine was a young woman of 33 years who had lived at home with her mother and stepfather until her early twenties. Since that time she had lived in residential care quite locally to her family. Her mother visited her regularly at weekends and seemed to be a very important constant in Catherine's life. At the beginning of her interview, Catherine found it difficult to think clearly about saying goodbye to particular keyworkers, because she had experienced so many losses of staff:

> *Lots of keyworkers round here ... Lucy then Anna, then Mary. Anna – she left, and Lucy, she's left ... she went on holiday herself – to Australia ... She was nice ... I didn't know [that she was leaving] ... I always talked to her down in this office. I am thinking about her [smiles] ... Sometimes I cried my eyes out [when she left] ... She sends me postcards. I like that – from Australia ... She had to leave – she had a job.*

When we asked Catherine whether she still thought about Lucy sometimes, she said:

> *Yes, but I don't cry my eyes out now – I used to. I was thinking to myself, my friend's died, and my father and my stepfather ... I don't like people leaving. It's serious ... I didn't want her to leave. I can't stand it ... And I miss Anna, too – because I loved Anna ... I always talked to her in the office ... I feel a bit tired when I'm thinking about it ... I get worried. I don't want staff leaving here.*

At the end of her interview, Catherine lamented mournfully over the loss of her keyworker, Anna: *I loved Anna ... I can't stand it,* indicating her sense of injustice that someone so special to her had been taken away.

Catherine's account seems to reflect her sense of loss and emotional pain after losing many keyworkers. Like Catherine, each of the clients we interviewed in our study identified feelings of hurt and sadness in the event of saying goodbye to staff.

Some clients, such as Jim, clearly articulated their feelings of loss and grief about saying goodbye to a keyworker:

> *I felt lost from here on ... hurtful, very hurtful ... It was like saying 'I may see you in the future, but I've got to go', sort of thing. 'I know we've been friends but now it's time to sever our friendship.' I felt gutted, you know, I felt really – I mean heaven only knows where I go from here ... It was hard, because she was one of my special friends, you know. And we got a sort of close relationship going. It was over a course of time that we got to know each other ...*

A few clients commented on the impact of saying goodbye as though they recognised that people might not notice or recognise their real and painful feelings.

Bill expressed this succinctly: *You can be sad without crying actually*.

Others described more hidden or private expressions of mourning, which were not easy to express. For example, Nick said: *When I was alone, I laid down and cried my eyes out. Sometimes it gets all bottled up.* Nick went on to describe his feelings about losing George, his recent keyworker:

> *I miss George, he played the drums, he played the drums, right. I miss – you know, it feels inside you right, you know what I mean. It feels inside you. I feel that here inside me. Then Colin comes along. He used to keywork me for a long time, and then Alison, and then Geoff and now Jim … I said to Mary, 'Who is my new keyworker?' She said, 'It's Jim', and I didn't know. I didn't know because he didn't tell me he would be my keyworker and then he did. He didn't know what my skills were. I'm upset all the people leaving.*

For Nick, there was a sense that his feelings were quite overwhelming. They were difficult to put into words. Perhaps he was also expressing a sense of feeling invisible, or feeling empty and void inside. These feelings may have been connected with Nick's uncertainties and fears about someone taking George's place and not knowing him.

Early on in our study, we noticed that several clients talked about physical or concrete manifestations of their emotional reactions to separation. We therefore incorporated into subsequent interviews some questions about where the clients physically located their feelings.

Diana related her sadness about losing her keyworker to sleep problems: *I can't sleep because Harriet has gone. If I want to go to sleep, I might have hot drinks make me put back to sleep.* In response to being asked where she felt the pain, Diana responded with certainty: *Upset stomach, pains in stomach.*

Eve recalled: *[I] feel it in my eyes.*

Catherine reported feeling tired and having a headache just thinking about saying goodbye.

Lilly's reaction to losing her keyworker seemed to be tied up with the loss of her mother and her perception of related physical reactions to grief:

> *She [the keyworker] had to leave, 'cause the other one had to as well. There was another keyworker. It was something to do with her job ... We had to give her a present. She said to us that she wanted to go away and she went just like that. She wanted to leave ... I said goodbye to her and she was gone. Then I saw her again twice in church. She said hello to me and I was sad because I lost my mum. She died and I had to be taken away because I was always with her, and I was upset and I had all this down my side. [Lilly pointed to the side of her body which had lost its functioning as a result of a stroke.]*

Lilly's account suggests that, in her own mind, her stroke was connected with her shock and grief following her mother's death – which had occurred shortly after her keyworker's departure. Lilly cried during the interview as she recounted her memories of her mother's death. Later on in the interview, Lilly told us how she felt when she thought about her keyworker:

> *I have a funny feeling – a cold feeling, something hits me – like when my friend died. She went just like that.*

The clients described here displayed something of their awareness that others might not necessarily recognise their emotional pain, especially if they were not grieving in the usual way. They may have found it difficult to express their pain and grief in terms of abstract feelings, but they were able to draw insightful links between their physical or somatic symptoms and their reactions to separations and loss. Although there were variations in how clients expressed the loss and grief they felt following separations from keyworkers, each one of the clients we interviewed described feelings of sadness, hurt and pain arising from this event.

Helplessness

> *It's difficult when someone leaves – it means there's a gap to fill, and it may take some time to fill that gap. And it's hard – It's hard because in theory it will all deject on to the clients I suspect.*

Interviewer: How does it feel when you think about having a new keyworker?

> *It does worry me, because it means having to make a fresh start with someone else that I don't know their philosophies. They may have other ideas as to how to go around a problem – I don't know.* (Jim)

Jim seemed to be very familiar with the process of losing a keyworker. There was a sense of this being a repeated and cyclical experience for him, as it is for many clients living in residential care. Adults with learning disabilities are constantly faced with having to struggle to begin new relationships with staff within the cyclical process of staff change and movement. There is an inevitability about their separations from keyworkers. The clients in this study described their anxieties about having no one left to care for them. However much they wanted to hold on to these relationships, they were powerless in the face of staff's decisions to leave, often without much warning, and sometimes never to return again.

Molly was quite preoccupied with why her keyworker, Louise, had decided to leave. Louise was pregnant and had recently left the residential home. In Chapter 5 we referred to the feelings that this may have evoked for Molly, who may have wanted to have a child of her own and who had lost contact with her own family. Another staff member, Harriet, had also left the home due to a family bereavement, a short time prior to our study. Molly was looking for some answers. She wanted ideas about how to bring staff back after they leave:

> *If a staff left, how do we bring them back? Good idea! Because Louise is having a baby, and when Louise's had the baby, she's coming out of hospital, she's having a rest, and when the baby grows up she might come here with the baby to visit ... and Harriet [another staff member] has gone home – to her place, 'cause her husband died ... When her husband died she didn't want to come back. I was upset because her husband died – because the staff know how to cheer people up.*

Diana lived in the same house as Molly and she too lamented the fact that Harriet had left the home. Diana seemed less able than Molly and she was quite repetitive in her speech. She seemed quite stuck on certain questions during our interview and at times we struggled to understand each other. Nevertheless, Diana was articulate and clear about her sense of hopelessness and disappointment about losing Harriet:

> *It was sad news ... I want her back. She said no – can't come back 'cause her husband died ... We write her a card, write her a letter, tell her she must come back. She don't want to come back, she's not bothered. Sometimes, if I haven't got a keyworker, I have to try and find a new keyworker. I miss Harriet.*

Whatever angry feelings Diana may have had, they seemed to get lost in the reality of life going on for both the staff and the residents. Anger may have shifted to sadness and then to fears and worries about being cared for in the future.

There was also a sense of inevitability and helplessness in many of the clients' accounts of repeated experiences of being 'abandoned', as Eve suggests:

> ... Norah did the same thing [as a previous keyworker] ... She went on holiday around the world ... I thought, 'What's going on?' ... I was worrying about that my keyworker was going to change [again] ... That I was going to lose one keyworker, then getting another one, then getting a new one.

A recurring theme in the residents' accounts was their lack of control over retaining relationships with staff:

> I don't know why they have to leave when I don't want them to – they have to. (Sally)

> I'm sad 'cause Julia will leave – I'm upset. [Audrey shouted out.] I don't know why she has to leave, because I don't want her to. But Julia does – not me, just Julia ... I am sad. I don't want to hurt her, because she's upset – Julia ... makes me feel sad, just sad. (Audrey)

Guy was one of many clients who described his longing for staff to return: *I wish her back*. This longing was often expressed with a painful realisation that there was nothing one could do to change the situation. It was out of the clients' control, as Diana indicated: *She can't come back – can't make it.*

However, a few clients seemed to have developed a fantasy of control over seeing their keyworker again. As Audrey put it: *She [the previous keyworker] will return if I want her to.* Similarly, Molly spoke as if she could control what was, in reality, an inevitable process of eventual separation from staff:

> *He's my keyworker and he's going to stick with me all the time, and he's not going to leave me. No – I like him very much.*

The theme of helplessness was also apparent in the clients' accounts of being passed around the staff team. As discussed in Chapter 5, there were times when keyworkers may have changed roles but were physically on site, and it was no longer appropriate for the residents to approach them because they had been allocated new keyworkers. This was the case with Jim, who seemed wistful about his close relationship with his previous keyworker and unsure about how to handle the new situation:

> *I can't confide in my old keyworker. It's a different relationship. He'll pass it on to my new keyworker ... it is hard to understand.*

A potential contributing factor to this condition of helplessness is suggested by Perske (1972, cited in Craft and Craft, 1981), who claims that systems of residential care are not good at enabling people to become more self-sufficient and to assume more personal responsibility. This idea is supported by the finding in the present study that clients were very dependent on staff for support, comfort and reassurance. Although people with learning disabilities spend much of their time in the company of large groups of people, the nature of the service setting can create an isolating environment. In their analysis of staff–client interactions, Clegg et al. (1991) question how much encouragement is given to

residents to support one another rather than to seek help
and support from staff.

Acceptance and Acquiescence

Although the clients expressed feelings of helplessness
about staff departures, they also recounted their experiences of becoming accustomed to the process of loss and
change. As Sally put it: *It was hard for me, but I got used
to it.* This 'acceptance' seemed to have developed after
repeated experiences of loss resulting in clients' withdrawal from the possibility of being hurt again in the
future. In general, many clients were aware of the possibility of keyworkers leaving, and their reactions were a
mixture of anticipation, worry, fear and a numbness to
the whole experience. Perhaps they were defending
against their more painful feelings by 'getting on' and
not surrendering to the pain:

I don't cry my eyes out any more. I used to. (Catherine)

*You, you get used to it – having someone new ... I still get
on [with a previous keyworker, who continued to work in
the house], but – we're getting some new staff soon.* (Eve)

Occasionally clients displayed their capacity to draw
on inner resources and private memories of relationships
with staff, to assist them in coping with their loss:

I have a picture of her ... I think what she was like.
(Sally)

However, for some clients, even their strategies for
coping with these losses were dependent on staff – for
reassurance, care and support:

I might talk to staff about Harriet coming back. (Diana)

The staff told me [I was upset]. I get the staff to calm me down. (Molly)

In Molly's case, her reliance on staff was extended to the point of needing someone else to identify her own distress about the loss.

Many residents showed a depth of insight into the limitations of the keyworking role, and an appreciation (or justification) of staff's decisions to leave. For example, Bill's account movingly reflects his level of understanding of the keyworker's needs. His keyworker, Sue, had left quite suddenly and it had been a shock to Bill. Nevertheless, he was able to offer a sensitive explanation for Sue's decision to move away. Throughout his account, Bill emphasised the need to 'make things nice' and enjoy the ending, because of a danger or prohibition against talking about the more painful aspects of saying goodbye:

She wanted to do a job where she didn't have to do shifts – because when she was doing shifts, she was getting very tired, and when you are very tired I don't think it's a good idea to start driving a car. Because when you are very tired you can't concentrate ... Gary told me that Sue was leaving. He said, 'I'm sorry, I have bad news for you, Sue is leaving', a few weeks before she left. I didn't want to talk to Sue about it because it would make her sad, because I just want to enjoy – I can still be her friend ... I asked why she was leaving and she told me, but I didn't go on about it ... because I think if you go on about something, it upsets the person ... I felt sad.

For Bill, talking to Sue about his sadness at her impending departure seemed dangerous: he feared that it would be too upsetting for her (and possibly for himself, as well). Furthermore, revealing his feelings about Sue to other staff seemed dangerous to Bill. When we asked him what he thought might happen if he talked about his feelings to staff members in his home, he told us of his fears that he would be prohibited from keeping in touch with Sue:

> *Well I don't know – the staff would take steps to not let me write to her any more ... if for some reason they said, 'Don't write to Sue any more, you are not to write to Sue any more', I would be sad and I would cry. Because I used to see a staff member called Vanessa, and they stopped me and I cried a lot. They weren't very kind where I lived then ... All I want to say is that I hope Gary [Bill's new keyworker] won't stop me writing to Sue ... If I cuddled her and kissed her and that kind of thing, then she would stop all ties with me ... You mustn't cuddle staff here – that's the policy. Even if they are upset. They wouldn't cuddle you if you were upset. They would just put a hand on you and talk to you and say, 'What's the matter?'*

Bill had clearly experienced quite intense feelings about particular keyworkers in the past, and he had been reminded that there were boundaries in the relationships between clients and staff that could not be transgressed.

Like Bill, Lilly showed an understanding of some of the factors which led her keyworker to leave. She had observed her keyworker, Rosie, suffering from some sort of harassment by the manager of her home:

> *I miss Rosie a lot – I like her. I wish she was my keyworker now ... it's sad. It was the manager, he's left now. When we went away [speaks in a quiet voice] he came with us. I remember Rosie got angry with him. She didn't like it – he used to put his arms round her. She was crying – I remember [Lilly started to cry as she spoke] ... I think she's gone to work somewhere else. I would love to see her. She liked me, she liked me.*

Lilly had obviously noticed something that was difficult for Rosie. Perhaps her own feelings of sadness in relation to losing Rosie were compounded by her sense of not being able to help her keyworker.

Some clients displayed their ability to acknowledge the reality of having to share the keyworker in the face of the staff's wider obligations to their own families. Notably, in several of the residential homes, keyworkers had left – or were about to leave – because of pregnancy (as Molly described above). Lilly, like Molly, recognised the keyworker's needs in this situation: *She has maternity leave – she will need to feed her baby.*

This appreciation of the personal lives of keyworkers sometimes included an acknowledgement of losses in the lives of staff. For example, Harry told us:

> *Graham [Harry's previous keyworker] has got a mother and son. Then his mum passed away, then funeral, me I couldn't go – oh no. Graham's friends … Very sad. He wasn't happy here. He was all right and then he left after that.*

Harry's comments indicate his awareness of his keyworker's sadness and also allude to his wish to support his keyworker, although there was no expectation or opportunity to do so. It was not expected or suggested that Harry might go to Graham's mother's funeral to support his keyworker. Harry knew that Graham had other people in his life who could support him at that time. This may have reinforced his awareness of the limitations of reciprocity and mutual support in his relationships with staff.

The clients' capacity for understanding sometimes extended to a consideration of the staff's feelings about saying goodbye. Jim was very articulate about how both he and his keyworker found it difficult to talk about their feelings regarding the keyworker's impending departure:

It was hard for both of us to express ... it's hard for them [staff], there is nothing easy about saying goodbye.

Diana, too, reflected on her keyworker's feelings: *She [the keyworker] felt sad to leave.* Sometimes, however, it was difficult to ascertain whether these reflections were based on insight, or whether they were projections of the residents' own feelings about saying goodbye to keyworkers. Audrey's comment about how she thought her keyworker, Julia, reacted to leaving perhaps reflects this muddle around the ownership of feelings: *I just know she's missing me – she'll be upset.* And yet it seemed hard for Audrey to stay with the more painful feelings about separating from Julia; she tried very hard to reassure us that everything would be fine:

I'll miss her – miss Julia. Because when she goes she's got a new job and that's it. I feel sad Julia's leaving – I will miss her. Hard feelings. Something new takes her place, something nice. Be OK.

Audrey seemed to be trying to persuade us that there was a positive side to Julia's leaving. Perhaps she was repeating what a member of staff had told her, or maybe she was protecting us – and herself – from her more painful and difficult feelings of sadness.

This sense of the danger of sad feelings, coupled with compliance, was apparent in many of the clients' descriptions. Guy put it very simply: *My sadness might hurt her.* Another client, Lilly, suggested that sadness and feelings of fondness were somehow incompatible: *I don't feel sad because I like her.* Taken to an extreme, this wish to please or protect the staff seems to negate the residents' realisations of their own rights to experience sadness.

Harry also hinted at his sense of his own feelings being unacceptable and destructive to staff. He talked about his sadness and not being 'nasty' in the same breath:

I do miss him now ... We were friends – talking and laying the table here for dinner. It is hard. I'm not nasty.

However, another way of interpreting Harry's comment is that it reflects a socially appropriate and emotionally mature response to his sadness. Many of us have difficult feelings about saying goodbye to people who are important in our lives and yet we will not express those feelings for fear of upsetting others. Instead, we may 'bite our lips' and put our own feelings aside to wish someone well for the future.

What struck us about so many of the clients' accounts was an implicit sense of compliance and an absence of anger. It may have been difficult, emotionally, for clients to think about how staff's personal situations drew them away from their keyworking roles. The clients may not have had only angry feelings about the separations, but also envious feelings when they considered the lives and opportunities of staff, which differed so much from their own. These emotions were not expressed, although they may have contributed to the emotional pain so often experienced by clients. The clients' accounts give a sense that they 'can't bite the hand that feeds them': a fear perhaps that if they do get angry, they might not receive any support. Given their circumstances, that is, being highly dependent on staff, this attitude seems eminently reasonable.

The absence of anger in clients' accounts can also be conceptualised from a psychodynamic point of view. Sinason (1992) argues that people with learning disabilities have difficulty expressing anger, rage or frustration because of a reluctance to feel consciously how unfair it is that they have learning disabilities. She suggests that people with learning disabilities often present themselves in ways which are inoffensive and easy going, 'for fear of offending those they are dependent on' (Sinason, 1992,

p. 21). The 'handicapped smile' – the apparently friendly, happy demeanour of handicapped people – thus disguises underlying feelings of sadness and insecurity.

CHAPTER 7

Feelings After Leaving: Staff's Stories

I mean you could say it's like a bereavement in a way. For Margaret it was a bereavement and for myself as well, really. I mean you've lost a good friend, haven't you? ... You know, when I first saw her at the club afterwards, I was really sort of choked up, and wanted to know all about her. Is she going on holiday? Is she doing this? Is she doing that? And you sort of feel, 'Well I could be organising that.'

Gill[1] had been working in residential care for five years at the time of our study. This quote is taken from her description of her relationship with Margaret, the first client she had been keyworker for. Gill had enjoyed a close relationship with Margaret for four years. She described Margaret as a very able older woman who responded to Gill's care and support with a maternal sensitivity and attachment. Margaret wanted to take care of Gill when she felt ill or tired: she wanted to look after her keyworker. She seemed to relish the time they spent together. Gill explained that Margaret communicated her feelings verbally, but sometimes displayed quite disturbed behaviour when angry or frustrated. Gill decided to leave Margaret and the home for a new job, and she spent two months preparing Margaret for their separation.

In the months following her departure, Gill often wondered how Margaret was. Gill was actually in a position to maintain quite regular contact with

---

1. The full interview with Gill is presented in Appendix D as an example of an interview with a staff member.

Margaret, because she continued to collect new clients
from the same day centre as Margaret attended (a
common situation for staff and clients). However, Gill
was advised to withdraw from Margaret for a while:

> *My former manager advised me it would be an idea to
> withdraw for a little while and then go back and visit, to
> give her time to get used to me going ... so [after I had left]
> I withdrew for about three months, and there was a club
> that Margaret went to every Wednesday night, and I
> walked into the club and this lady [Margaret] ran from
> the other end of the club just shouting my name from one
> end to another. So you know, it was quite difficult for her.
> She did used to attach herself. But then, as I say, she did
> used to shout for members of staff that she had known
> years ago, years before.*

We asked Gill about her understanding of Margaret's
reaction to her departure and the end of their
keyworking relationship. Gill had remained in contact
with some of the other staff at Margaret's home who
reported regularly on Margaret's progress and her
response to her new keyworker:

> *Apparently she became very withdrawn. Her repetitive
> speech became more, a very articulate lady but when
> people spoke to her she would start to switch off and start
> doing the 'Where's my duvet?', all the repetitive stuff.
> Then she started coming round and becoming attached to
> another member of staff ... I think she's been in care for so
> long that she's learned that people will probably go through
> her life and leave ... that there's going to be lots of people
> going through her life.*

Interviewer: You mentioned that she had attached
herself to another member of staff. I wonder how that
made you feel?

A little bit jealous, yes, a little bit jealous. But then again relief, because then you knew she was OK, because she did need that support and somebody to talk to really.

Gill had mixed feelings about Margaret's adjusting to someone else. Gill herself had lost an important role and felt usurped by Margaret's new keyworker. Perhaps these feelings can be compared to a parent's experience of a child leaving home and moving away to start a new life. The parent knows that the child must develop her own independence and new adult relationships, but often has mixed feelings all the same.

Gill recognised Margaret's regression, both immediately after hearing the news that Gill was leaving and in the aftermath of being told. Gill was also aware of her own depth of feeling about Margaret and her need to keep in touch with her and to hear about how things were for her at home:

I kept thinking about her, and also being very tempted to sort of visit. If you drove near the home, you'd feel like knocking and saying, 'Can I go in and visit Margaret?'... it was very tempting to ring up and say, 'Is it all right to go in and visit Margaret?'

Gill also reflected on the wider phenomenon of staff turnover in residential homes and how this affects clients:

... staff turnover in some residential homes is so high that it's devastating really. There were some residents – one particular lady there who didn't become attached to anybody, she just totally switched off, because she had probably got a tough exterior. She had been in care since she was five, so she had developed this tough exterior, thinking, 'If I get attached to somebody, they're going to up and go.' So she never got attached to anybody, she was just for herself – let's put it that way.

Gill's account provides a useful starting place for exploring the feelings about separation for keyworker and client alike. Not all of the staff we interviewed indicated their own feelings of grief and loss at the end of the keyworking relationship, but Gill was aware of her attachment to Margaret and of her own investment in their relationship.

This chapter focuses on staff's feelings about leaving clients. It also includes their perceptions of the residents' feelings and reactions to their departures. The chapter is organised around three central themes: attachment and separation, denial, and self-devaluation.

Attachment and Separation

Despite the boundaries and limitations of their roles, staff in residential settings often develop strong emotional attachments to residents. These attachments may differ in form and intensity from the experiences of residents (as indicated by the staff's descriptions of the keyworking role – see Chapter 4), but they are nevertheless evident. They may result in the staff's sentiments of loss, guilt or remorse in the event of saying goodbye to clients.

Like Gill, many staff were open and honest about their own painful feelings (and their perceptions of the impact on clients); in many ways their feelings mirrored those of the clients they described. Nevertheless, the staff's accounts suggested that they had not anticipated the extent of their own painful feelings and the element of co-dependency which may emerge within the staff–client relationship. For example, Nia expressed surprise at the strength of her feelings after leaving her client, Scott:

I really do miss him [Scott] and I have found that after a horrendous day here, my automatic reaction will be to go there [her previous workplace]. I don't even think to myself that I'll just pop in. I'm just driving and then suddenly I find I'm on that road.

When Nia left her old workplace to take up the position of manager in a new home, she was still very attached to Scott. Scott was a 40-year-old man who was loud and chatty and had a strong personality. Before taking up her new post, Nia stayed in the home for a short time but relinquished her responsibilities as a keyworker; this was clearly a very difficult transition for her. She found herself continuing to care specifically for Scott: cutting his hair, supporting him with cooking and shopping, and generally spending more time with him than other clients. She would then confide guiltily in his new keyworker that she had taken on some of his responsibilities:

> *It was strange, little things like haircuts. It was almost like I would just do it, and then I would think, 'Oh no, I'm not supposed to do that.'*

Nia described her visits to the day centre to collect her new clients, where she often saw Scott. It seemed to be very painful for both of them to be reminded of one another. Nia's account powerfully communicates the tangled grief of staff and residents that results from losing a reciprocally important relationship:

> *It is very hard, and I think that what makes it harder is that I do still see him. I think that if I had moved right away from the area, and never saw him, it would have hit me, but it wouldn't have dragged out. I suppose it's almost like losing a boyfriend. I spent more time with Scott than I would have done with a boyfriend ...*

Alice was another keyworker who reflected on her sadness about leaving her client, Sally. Not long ago Alice had taken over from someone else as Sally's keyworker, and at the time of our study she had just informed Sally that she too was leaving. Alice was worried about their impending separation, but tried to reassure herself that she would soon be replaced and forgotten:

> *I think I'll miss Sally terribly and I feel that, I think she's going to miss me being there for her ... But I think if she gets another keyworker who will work with her closely, and who will be sensitive, I think she'll be OK. I think the loss of me will soon go away, I do believe that ... I mean I don't know how deep it goes for Sally, I mean I can only speak for me. When we are together sometimes, what she says, it really feels genuine. I will miss her ... But if she gets somebody else that will be able to do the things that I do with her in the same way, she'll be fine. I don't think it will take her long to forget that I existed.*

Alice also seemed to be questioning here whether Sally's feelings about her were genuine. This may reflect her own uncertainty about her role as a keyworker and her importance to the client. However, there may also have been a sense of wanting to deny her own significance to Sally. We shall return to this idea when we discuss the theme of denial later in this chapter.

Nicola's account of her separation from her client, Susan, illustrates some of the powerful feelings of guilt and personal responsibility that staff may experience towards clients:

> *When I told her I was leaving it was an emotional thing for both of us. I remember her crying an awful lot and she actually detached herself from me before I left. She didn't want to talk to me, and she really reverted back to how she had been. And that made me think, 'Oh gosh, I shouldn't be going, I'm letting her down, she's gone backwards and it's all my fault.'*

Nicola recalled the day that she had first told Susan she was leaving to go travelling. She had promised to write and stay in touch. Susan's response was quite immediate:

> *She just looked at me with these eyes, and I just remember the brown eyes looking at me, thinking, 'What have I done?' And she just threw herself at me and she hugged me for a while, and I said, 'Can you understand what I have just said?' And she said, 'Yes, you're going.' ... I remember her crying an awful lot, and she actually detached herself from me before I left. She didn't want to talk to me and really reverted back to how she had been.*

Nicola explained that, for Susan, the news of her imminent departure was completely unexpected. Susan was obviously distressed about the thought of losing her keyworker, and she reacted by withdrawing into herself. Nicola felt punished by her client's silent reaction, and at times Nicola seemed to feel she deserved that punishment. On the day of Nicola's departure, Susan finally broke her silence:

> *Until the actual day that I left she didn't talk very much, and then the day that I left she spoke to me and she hugged me and cried, and told me that she would miss me and she told all the other residents ... I think once I had explained to her why I was going, I think she was upset, but I think she understood.*

Nicola came back to work with Susan two years later, having had intermittent contact in between. Shortly before she returned, Nicola went to the house to celebrate Susan's birthday. She was then in the unusual position of being able to witness the impact of their separation:

She [Susan] invited me to her party, and I came along, and she just hugged me for an hour [laughs]. She had like her family and friends around, but she just stood there at the door hugging me. It was quite sweet, but it was quite emotional.

Interviewer: Did you feel emotional as well?

Yes, but I kept saying, 'Silly woman', and trying to be jovial about it.

Interestingly, it seemed to be the keyworker, not the client, in this instance who had difficulty tolerating the emotional pain of coming back together after their long separation.

Later in our interview, Nicola also recalled the time when she had gone on holiday for two weeks and had forgotten to mention it to Susan:

When I came back, she wouldn't talk to me ... and apparently the whole two weeks she was very quiet and very withdrawn and stuff, and I just couldn't work out why, and when I came back she would not talk to me – no contact at all. And I said, 'I've been on holiday, did you not receive my postcard?' And it turned out she hadn't, and it arrived three days later ... I don't think anybody had, I mean the fact that I hadn't told her ... she probably felt very deserted.

Nicola had experienced at first hand the traumatic impact on her client of even a very brief separation. The profound impact of such separations may reflect residents' anxieties and uncertainties about the permanence of relationships in their lives. These anxieties are not surprising, in view of many residents' lifelong history of institutional care and transient relationships with carers.

Some of the staff in our study expressed a sense of their own indispensability, voicing concerns that replacement staff might fail to recognise the residents' needs. They feared that their own departure might cause permanent damage to, or regression in, clients. For these staff, their awareness of the residents' possible reactions, coupled with their own painful feelings, often led to guilt and worry:

I worry about her maintaining her skills. (Alice)

I worried that the next person to step in to my shoes would not be so patient. (Pete)

Many of the keyworkers recognised and appreciated the residents' feelings about impending separations:

She was quite sad, she knew I was going. And sometimes I think she was quite angry as well, because she knew she was a resident and I was a staff member and it was going to happen – but it had happened so many times before. (Barbara)

Tilly was just really shocked, and she said to me, 'I'm really shocked.' (Charlotte)

I used to say to him, 'Dan, I'm going to be leaving', and he would sort of look at me and then he'd say, 'Can you lift me up, or prop me up you know' [laughs] if he was falling over and stuff. But I could have said to him a week later and he would say, 'Oh no, why?' ... At the time I just thought, 'Oh he don't care' ... I must admit I haven't thought about that until now ... it does sound sad when you think about it though [laughs nervously]. You don't think about it as much when you are working all the time though. (Rob)

For Rob, the process of reflecting on his role and relationship with Dan had allowed him to think more clearly
about the impact of his departure on the client.
Sometimes it can be difficult for staff to think about this
at the time, and their own reactions to separation may
consequently be delayed as well.

When clients have difficulties in verbally expressing
their emotions, it can be hard for staff to recognise their
reactions to separation. Alice described this problem to
us. She had observed how Sally had reacted to hearing
the news that her keyworker, Emily, was going to leave
(Alice's account of this is presented in Chapter 5). Sally
had yelled and screamed upon first being told, but she
was unable to verbally articulate her feelings of grief.
Alice knew that Sally was upset; however, she was
uncertain about Sally's longer-term reaction to Emily's
departure. Alice expressed some puzzlement about
clients' reactions to loss:

> There may be a process of grief, but I don't see it. I'm
> saying that whether it's internalised, I don't know – I
> don't see it in their behaviour. I don't see it and they don't
> verbalise it, you know. You don't see people going through
> this process of grief.

Staff sometimes noticed clients' more implicit, behavioural expressions of grief, such as regressive or
withdrawn behaviour. For example, Maria described her
client's withdrawn behaviour in reaction to hearing
about her departure:

> His behaviour changed. Throughout that week he never
> opened his mouth. He used to sit in the corner and have
> his lunch on his own.

Maria had experienced difficulties in saying goodbye
when she left her previous place of work. She had

received little support from her manager and had given her client four days' notice of her departure. During those four days, her client had stopped talking to her completely. In her new place of work, however, Maria seemed to draw on her past experiences of observing clients' varied (and often delayed) responses to separations from staff who had been significant in their lives:

There are tears and sadness and anxieties and worry ... who [which staff member] will go next and will they be doing this or that. But it's quite good because the member of staff is always talked about. The pictures are taken out, especially if you know that someone is looking quite down ... One resident in particular goes and gets his pictures, and you say, 'Do you want to phone?' And they say, 'Yes.' So that's his way of telling us that he is feeling a bit down, so we are able to pick up on that and help him.

Like Maria, several keyworkers we interviewed noted how they had learned lessons from being with residents in the aftermath of a change in keyworker. They had observed not only the more obvious, verbal expressions of grief, but also the more subtle signs, such as withdrawal. These observations helped them to think about and plan for future separations.

Denial

As we have seen above, recognising clients' distress following (or in anticipation of) loss can be emotionally painful for staff. For some staff members in our study, the painful reality of their own importance to clients seemed difficult to tolerate. This appeared to lead to a process of denying or defending against clients' loss and distress, and failing to acknowledge clients' less obvious communications of grief. Sometimes, of course, a client may not be negatively affected by a keyworker's departure (not all keyworking relationships are good). However, striking inconsistencies in some of the staff's accounts suggested a process of denial: they talked perceptively about clients' distress at one moment and then disavowed it at the next.

Such inconsistencies were apparent in Ben's recollections of his client, Hugh:

When I told him I was going he sort of went, 'Oh no, don't want to talk about it, don't want to talk about it' – and he reverted to that sort of childlike behaviour ... He cried a couple of times on the day that I was leaving, but again it's hard to know whether it's sincere crying because that's the thing to do, or whether he does really have feelings and emotions ...

But history and past philosophies was that when staff left, they didn't tell residents. They just went, they were replaced the following day by someone else. For years I think that was the case in the home. And Hugh would just not talk about it, but obviously – staff leaving – it is a bereavement and he doesn't really talk to me now [when I go back].

Interviewer: What was your impression, when you were saying it's hard to know how sincere it is?

I don't know, I think deep down he was sorry I was going. But the fact that he bawled his eyes out considerably, and it was his pattern of behaviour sort of thing, it wasn't necessarily genuine. He was upset that I was leaving, but he over-reacted almost. To the point that he became very, very childlike ... I had to talk to him a couple of times – when he was really upset – he would come running in to the building, put his arms round me and hug me ... he said, 'I'm upset', and on a couple of occasions, 'I don't want you to go' ... I still think that the majority of his being upset is probably because it is the done thing, that's what you are supposed to do.

Ben alternated between recognising the impact of his departure on Hugh and questioning the sincerity of Hugh's reaction. It was almost as though he could not believe the extent of his own importance to his client. Perhaps it was too difficult for him to tolerate the level of emotion Hugh displayed. It seemed easier for Ben to acknowledge the impact of separation when he was not personally involved:

> *I have been in some homes where a keyworker has left and the client has dealt with it fine. But eight months down the line something has triggered it off, and that is the result of the fact that eight months ago their keyworker left. You may be dealing with a behavioural problem later and you don't know why they are doing it. That is often because it has taken them that long for them suddenly to get it out of their system and deal with it.*

As Ben noted, clients' reactions to staff departures may not be immediately obvious. Furthermore, clients are not always able to verbally articulate their distress, but may express it in their behaviour.

A recurring theme in many staff's accounts was their perception that residents were almost unaffected by the loss of their keyworking relationship. Various views and explanations were put forward. In some cases the staff seemed to have difficulty recognising the feelings of residents, or assumed that people with learning disabilities do not have the capacity to grieve. In other cases the staff seemed to underestimate their own importance to residents, or believed that people with learning disabilities become 'numb' to the experience of loss in their lives.

Oliver found it difficult to attribute emotional reactions
to his client, Simon – despite obvious manifestations of
distress:

> *He [Simon] went downhill after that [Oliver's departure].*
> *He was putting on weight just as I left and his epilepsy got*
> *worse. He probably had two bad years after I left ... his*
> *mum connects that with me going. But I mean it*
> *[epilepsy] always gets worse for a while and then you*
> *change the medication and it gets better again.*

Interviewer: So you don't make any connection between the change in Simon and the fact that you left?

> *No, but there definitely was a change.*

Oliver seemed to find it hard to even consider a link
between his departure and Simon's worsening
symptoms of epilepsy. At one point during our interview, he reflected on the importance of his relationship
with Simon (and other clients), yet moments later he
seemed to express contradictory feelings:

> *I do tend to get emotionally involved with clients, I really*
> *do, because I think empathy is one of the best things you*
> *can give to a client ... Well, Simon's 45 now, say he's*
> *been in care for 42 years, he has probably had a new*
> *keyworker every 2 years, so he's probably had 20*
> *keyworkers ... I don't know ... all this empathy and all*
> *the rest of it – I don't think clients really, I don't know*
> *how much they miss you.*

Interestingly, Oliver drew a parallel between Simon's life
and his own experience of working abroad:

> *I mean it's like, well I used to work abroad, so I've got a*
> *weird perception of relationships because 16 years' working*

*abroad – you'd meet people who were out on 2-year contracts
and then they'd be gone. So I really was in the same situation as clients, thinking, 'It's nice meeting you, we've had
some really good fun, bye now.'*

Some keyworkers seemed to underestimate, or
minimise, their own importance to residents, perhaps in
an unconscious effort to avoid thinking about the potential impact of their departure. For example, Alex seemed
to have a very good understanding of his former client,
Frank. In Chapter 5, we described how Alex had
regretted not telling Frank that he was leaving, after
another staff member had 'dived in' to say Alex was
going on holiday. Alex had been worried about the
impact of his departure on Frank. However, when we
asked Alex how he thought Frank had reacted, he told
us that Frank probably would have hardly noticed his
absence:

> *Strangely enough, I don't think Frank was too bothered
> … I'm not sure that he noticed too much, because there
> were so many people in that house anyway – he may have
> noticed that certain activities weren't happening, because
> there wasn't someone there to make sure that Frank went
> on them and to probably drive the bus …*
>
> *I get the feeling that he would probably notice that I
> wasn't there, would probably wonder where the guy was
> that helped him out in the mornings and used to pop along
> to the day centre, helped him out and talked to him.
> Because even though Frank wouldn't respond verbally,
> there were plenty of ways that he would, maybe he missed
> that. But as for an individual or a face, I'm not sure.*

At the time of leaving, Alex himself had been preoccupied with the level of violence amongst clients and the
risk to staff working at the home. He felt an overwhelming sense of relief after leaving Frank and the

other residents. Consequently it may have been hard for
him to think about, or tolerate, his client's feelings about
separation:

> All I felt was, 'Thank goodness I am out of that home and
> I haven't been seriously injured.' And that probably
> sounds melodramatic, but three weeks earlier I had been
> caught on my own in a room with a resident and he had
> tried to assault me, and then you are expected to work a
> shift.

Some staff had difficulty acknowledging that people
with learning disabilities can experience grief and
feelings of sadness about losing relationships. For those
staff who worked with adults with moderate or severe
learning disabilities, this was especially difficult. For
example, Tom assumed that his departure would have
no impact on his client, who displayed autistic behaviours:

> He probably won't be bothered like that – I could have
> been anyone. I did tell him I'm going, but he just carried
> on licking his fingers and staring at the wall ... I'm not
> sure he would have understood the concept of going. He
> was in his autistic world.

In this case Tom seemed to relate the client's 'diagnosis'
or 'syndrome' to an incapacity to experience emotions.
However, it is well-known that predictability and consistency are important for people with autism; and yet it
may be just these clients whose needs are lost or difficult
for staff to discern.

Other keyworkers 'explained away' the emotional
impact of separations with the suggestion that the residents had become used to the process. For example,
Barbara told us:

You see her kind of adapt when staff come and go, and it's like, 'OK here's another person' ... but she's probably just become accustomed to it all.

Having experienced many losses in their lives, residents may become hardened, or numbed, to the impact of losing keyworkers. Nevertheless, we would argue that further losses may still have an impact: numbness to feelings does not mean having no feelings at all. We will return to this issue in Chapter 8.

Self-devaluation

You felt that someone else could fill your shoes very easily, it wasn't necessarily that he would miss you as a person at all. (Alex)

The clients might miss the times [spent with a keyworker], but I mean they might not relate the times to the person ... (Oliver)

I mean he reacted to it the same as if anything was missing. I mean if you took away his old shoes because they were knackered and had holes in, he wouldn't like it. (Pete)

As we have noted above, staff often tended to minimise the importance of their roles and their personal relationships with clients. They often suggested that their departure did not matter to clients, as long as the clients' basic needs were met. And yet these same staff often indicated a sense of their own indispensability, as we saw earlier in this chapter: they feared that new staff would not be able to meet the clients' needs. Flipping between these opposite poles of dispensability and indispensability, staff sometimes seemed confused about what their relationships with clients meant.

The self-devaluation expressed by staff may reflect a process of internalising the devalued nature of their roles. Like the clients, staff are sometimes unthinkingly passed around the service. They may receive limited expressions of appreciation by clients and little recognition by managers of their contributions to the wider service. Furthermore, their work is not rewarded with high pay or social status.

Oliver expressed a sense that clients become used to having different staff and one is no different from the next:

> I think Simon had so many people in his life, you know, so many workers come in – hands-on care, I mean intimate care. I think a lot of clients just get fazed out. It's just part of life ... I don't think he missed me.

An implicit message in many of the staff's accounts was that anybody could fulfil the 'functional' role of the keyworker. Staff seemed to view themselves in a 'de-personalised' way, describing their roles rather than their personal characteristics or the personal nature of their relationships with residents. Some staff felt that they were filling a gap in the residents' lives, which anyone could fill. Over half of the staff we interviewed suggested that it was the times or the activities – rather than themselves as individuals – which the residents missed.

In the absence of an observable reaction in residents at the time of saying goodbye, some keyworkers reported 'discovering' the impact of their departures from other staff who had witnessed the residents' reactions. For example, Rob explained:

> I heard [from the remaining staff] that they [the residents] were very sad, and it made me feel quite good actually. Everyone needs a bit of appreciation, don't they?

These comments reflect Rob's reliance on others to remind him of his own value to the residents, as though he was unable to grasp an idea of his worth without some clear evidence or acknowledgement.

Other keyworkers expressed their discomfort with the sense of not being valued:

A hole in his life – can be filled by someone else. It felt as if I was on a conveyer belt, and someone else was going to come behind me and go through the exact same process. It was horrible. (Maria)

I think Oscar's anxiety was focused on who was going to come and replace me rather than my leaving ... I mean there is definitely a feeling of people being dependent on you, for certain things and for certain responses, and you know, for feedback, and I did feel like I was leaving all of them, and because there was no replacement that made me feel worse, definitely. (Lucy)

Being passed around services seemed to add to some staff's sense of being devalued. (Similarly, some clients hinted at feeling devalued as a result of being 'passed around' keyworkers.) As we mentioned in earlier chapters, team restructuring frequently meant that staff changed their role within a residential home, or moved to another home within the service. This resulted in keyworkers being asked to 'pass on' their clients to other staff members. This process seemed to impact on staff in various ways, ranging from difficult and jealous feelings to thoughts about the positive effects of change.

Karen talked about her own feelings of failure arising from being asked to change her role within the service:

I suppose I was disappointed, and maybe I felt a bit of a failure too at the time. I thought, 'Maybe you know, it's through me that I've got to move on', although I knew at

the time I was asked by the manager. But you do feel a bit
of a failure, you feel perhaps it could have been somebody
else that could have done it – although in my mind I
wasn't ready to move on.

However, some staff felt that change was positive and healthy for all concerned (although it might also have been painful). A common view was that the process of change allowed for new influences and fresh ideas, and prevented over-dependence in residents. Some staff felt strongly that this process eased the experience of eventual separation at the end of the keyworking relationship. Charlotte explained:

It's much better if people know from the outset that they
are going to be with a keyworker for 18 months – and
everyone knows then everyone is going to swap.

Although the process of changing keyworkers was sometimes managed successfully, many staff felt that more could be done by managers and staff teams to facilitate the process. As we indicated in Chapter 5, keyworkers often felt unsupported in thinking about how best to prepare their clients for change. This lack of support seemed to feed into the keyworkers' sense of their unimportance to clients. In Chapter 9 we discuss ways in which both keyworkers and clients might be supported during times of transition.

CHAPTER 8

Why is it Hard to Say Goodbye?

The truth shall make you free – but first it shall make you miserable.[1]

The accounts of clients and staff, presented in Chapters 4–7, indicate how difficult the process of saying goodbye can be. Clients vividly described their feelings of sadness and loss when keyworkers left. Sometimes they recalled the abrupt departures of keyworkers; given little or no preparation for the ending of the relationship, they were left bewildered and distressed. Many of the staff also described the endings of their relationships with residents as difficult and bewildering. They were often aware of the distress caused to clients by their own (or by a previous staff member's) departure, but felt confused and uncertain about saying goodbye – that is, when and how to tell residents they were leaving, or even whether advance warning and discussion would be helpful. Many delayed telling their clients until a few days before their departure, and a few described leaving without saying goodbye at all. Those who did prepare their clients often found the process of ending upsetting: they not only had to face the client's distress, but also their own feelings of letting the client down.

In this chapter, we draw together the themes which emerged from the stories told by clients and staff. We

---

1. The first part of this quotation is biblical, from John, 8:32. The second part seems to be of more recent origin. The whole quotation was taken from Shlien (1973), who describes it as being proverbial.

discuss these themes in the context of the research and theoretical literature reviewed in Chapter 2. In order to understand why the process of saying goodbye can be difficult, we first consider what the keyworker relationship meant for both residents and staff. We then examine how the endings of staff–client relationships were experienced, again from the viewpoints of both residents and staff. Finally, we discuss why staff may find it hard to say goodbye to clients and why the process of saying goodbye is important. We believe that, although endings can be emotionally painful, in the longer term it is usually better to address endings directly with clients, rather than avoid talking about them. As the quote at the beginning of this chapter suggests, facing the truth with clients, while difficult in the short term, can ultimately empower them to deal with the difficulties of life which we all encounter.

The Meaning of the Keyworker Relationship

One of the most striking themes from our interviews was the importance of the keyworker relationship to residents as well as staff. Residents often expressed great fondness for their keyworkers, who played a central part in their lives. Keyworkers, too, often developed strong attachments to residents – attachments which the keyworkers themselves did not always anticipate when they first started working in residential care.

Both the clients' and the staff's accounts indicated that keyworkers had a range of roles and types of relationships with their clients. This is consistent with previous studies of the roles of care staff (Allen et al., 1990; Clegg et al., 1996). In most instances, being a keyworker was not just about providing physical and practical care, but also involved the development of a personal relationship with the client. Keyworkers strove to make sense of the feelings and needs which clients had difficulty expressing themselves, they provided essential emotional support to clients, and they often became companions and friends in the absence of other close relationships. The intimacy of residential care work was reflected in how clients described staff, likening them to friends, family members or even partners in some cases.

Many staff described, sometimes with surprise, a sense of reciprocity and mutual pleasure in their relationships with residents. Staff and residents often enjoyed each other's company and appreciated each other as individuals. Like the residents, staff also described their relationships as being similar to those they had with friends and family members. Interestingly, although they often felt they took on the role of a parent, looking after the resident, at times they felt like a child, being looked after by an older resident.

Although the keyworker relationship was perceived in a variety of ways, a central theme running through the clients' accounts was their appreciation of the keyworker as someone who they could rely on and who had a long-term perspective of their needs. The keyworker was valued as a 'constant' in their lives: someone who knew their background and was aware of the particular care they needed. There was a fundamental sense of feeling 'known' by the keyworker, and the prospect of having to start all over again with a new keyworker therefore sometimes felt overwhelming. The importance which clients placed on the keyworker as a constant, stable figure in their lives is understandable in the context of many clients' histories, which commonly involve repeated losses and transient relationships (Allen et al., 1990; Clegg and Lansdall-Welfare, 1995).

Related to this idea of the keyworker as a 'constant' was an underlying theme of dependency. Both the clients' and the staff's accounts hinted at the issue of dependency, which seemed a core aspect of their relationships.

For clients, the keyworker was their provider and nurturer – their lifeline. The very existence of staff–client relationships of course means that one member is in need of, and dependent upon, the other. However, most adults with learning disabilities living in residential care will never gain full independence; rather, their dependency will shift from one staff member to another, only to be shifted again and again.

For staff, the residents' high levels of dependency often felt uncomfortable and overwhelming. This was not so much an issue of being relied on for physical or practical needs, but rather an issue of emotional dependence. Some staff members were acutely aware of how much they meant to clients on a personal level: they had developed close relationships in which they supported clients through the 'ups and downs' of their everyday lives. The closeness of such relationships frequently resulted in keyworkers feeling 'emotionally overloaded', as well as worrying about the loss the client might experience when their relationship eventually ended. Other keyworkers seemed to minimise or underestimate their importance to clients, perhaps as a way of protecting themselves from the uncomfortable feelings aroused by their clients' dependency. We return to staff's underestimation of their importance later in this chapter.

The Ending of the Keyworker Relationship

All of the residents we interviewed described painful feelings of sadness and loss arising from the departures of keyworkers. The accounts of staff were consistent with this: they had frequently observed how distressed residents were after a keyworker had left. Furthermore, the staff themselves often felt sad and upset when ending relationships with clients whom they had become fond of.

Historically, it has been assumed that people with learning disabilities cannot form close, emotional attachments to others and therefore they will not grieve following death or separation (Oswin, 1981; Yanok and Beifus, 1993). The stories from residents in our study clearly challenge this assumption. As we have already discussed, residents often formed close attachments to their keyworkers. It is not surprising, therefore, that the loss of these relationships led to a process of grieving. Clients themselves spontaneously made a link between losing a keyworker and losing a friend or family member through death: both experiences aroused similar feelings of grief.

The residents' reactions to the departures of staff can be understood in terms of typical reactions to bereavement. As Oswin (1981, 1991) and Harper and Wadsworth (1993) have pointed out, people with learning disabilities mourn and grieve in much the same way as other people do. Typical grief reactions include a mixture of sadness and depression, anxiety, anger and confusion (Harper and Wadsworth, 1993). Many of the clients clearly articulated their feelings of grief: they described 'crying my eyes out', feeling 'gutted' and 'hurt', and finding it difficult to tolerate the painfulness of being without someone they had felt close to. Some clients described physical reactions to grief, such as headaches and sleep problems. Others described hiding their feelings from those around them and mourning in private, perhaps because they found their feelings difficult to express or because they worried about how others would react. A few clients were aware that others might not recognise their feelings of grief, especially if they were not expressing these feelings openly or directly.

Expressing grief through words will be difficult for some people with learning disabilities. As Harper and Wadsworth's (1993) study of bereavement indicates, clients with limited verbal communication often express their grief through their behaviours, for example by hitting out or withdrawing. Some of the staff in our study recognised clients' behavioural expressions of distress, both immediately after hearing the news that keyworkers were leaving and in the aftermath of their departures. For example, staff noticed how clients regressed to lower levels of functioning, or withdrew completely from interactions with others. Other staff, however, were unaware of, or puzzled by, behavioural expressions of grief; they seemed to assume that, in the absence of obvious expressions of sadness, clients did not grieve. Again, this is consistent with studies of bereavement, which suggest that care staff often do not recognise the grief reactions of people with learning disabilities (Emerson, 1977; Oswin, 1981; Harper and Wadsworth, 1993). This failure to notice or understand clients' reactions to loss is likely to complicate the grieving process and lead to greater distress and behavioural problems (Oswin, 1981; Ghazziudin, 1988; Harper and Wadsworth, 1993).

The residents' descriptions of how they felt when keyworkers left rarely included feelings of anger, although anger is often considered to be a normal part of the grieving process (Parkes, 1972; Bowlby, 1980). Rather, the residents seemed compliant and accepting of staff departures. They described becoming accustomed to the process of loss and change: most had experienced repeated changes of staff and said that they 'got used to it'. Furthermore, they often seemed to appreciate keyworkers' own needs and reasons for leaving, such as obligations to their own families. Indeed, many residents showed quite a lot of insight into the nature of the keyworker role, recognising that it had certain boundaries and limits.

However, the residents' apparent acceptance of losing keyworkers may also have masked more uncomfortable feelings, such as anger and sadness. Several residents mentioned their fears of expressing their feelings, hinting at the potential dangerousness or destructiveness of doing so. As one client put it, *My sadness might hurt her [the keyworker]*. Kauffman (1994) echoes this idea, suggesting that clients may feel afraid not only of being hurt by staff abandoning them, but also of the power of their own words to hurt staff. As Sinason (1992) points out, it may be difficult for people with learning disabilities to express feelings such as anger or disappointment because of their fear of angering or offending people whom they depend on. Sinason thus argues that the 'happy face' of many clients does not express genuine happiness, but rather is intended to keep others happy. In this way, the residents' apparent acceptance of staff departures may have disguised underlying feelings of sadness and anger which sometimes felt too dangerous to express.

The clients' comments about becoming accustomed to staff changes had parallels in the staff's accounts. Several staff suggested that, having experienced so many losses in their lives, residents had become hardened, or 'numbed', to the impact of losing a keyworker. Sometimes it seemed that these staff were minimising, or discounting, the possibility of grief; they assumed that if the client did not appear distressed, she was not emotionally affected. Yet we know from what the clients told us that their grief was not always expressed openly. Rather than being numb to feelings of sadness, they often found these feelings difficult to tolerate and difficult to talk about. However, one serious consequence of repeated experiences of loss is that clients may not allow themselves to become close to people again – that is, it may feel too painful and risky to form an emotional attachment. Then, indeed, they may not be emotionally affected by staff changes.

A sense of helplessness and inevitability was also present in the clients' accounts of losing keyworkers. Many recounted the numerous staff changes they had experienced, naming each keyworker in succession;

some also talked about being passed around from one keyworker to another, even when the previous keyworker remained on site. There was a combination of longing and powerlessness in their descriptions of not being able to get in touch with keyworkers who had left and wishing they could 'make keyworkers come back again'. This sense of helplessness partly reflects the reality of clients' lives: staff come and go and clients have no control over this.

However, the way in which some keyworker relationships ended may have unnecessarily increased clients' feelings of helplessness. Learned helplessness theory (Seligman, 1975) provides a useful framework for understanding this. If people are frequently in situations over which they have no control, they learn to be helpless; that is, they come to expect that they cannot control events in their lives. Feelings of apathy and depression are a common outcome of learned helplessness. As Swain (1989) points out, people with learning disabilities usually have a long history of situations in which they lack control or choice; consequently they learn to feel helpless and powerless. Sudden departures of keyworkers are likely to reinforce clients' feelings of helplessness: a lack of preparation or warning will result in clients feeling even more powerless and unable to control their lives. Clients' apparent apathy and acquiescence in response to loss, which we have already noted, can also be understood as a consequence of this sense of powerlessness. Preparation for the endings of keyworker relationships can help clients to feel some sense of control, and thus seems of paramount importance.

Why is it Hard for Staff to Say Goodbye?

The staff in our study described a multitude of feelings about ending their relationships with clients. Many felt sad about leaving, much as they would if they were moving away from friends or family: they had become emotionally attached and, like the clients, experienced the ending as a loss. Sometimes they felt relief or excitement – relieved to be leaving a demanding and emotionally draining job, or excited about the prospects (such as a new job or a holiday) which lay ahead. Often they felt worried and guilty about leaving: they were aware of their clients' potential reactions to their departure and they felt bad about letting them down or abandoning them. Understandably, these feelings were often uncomfortable for staff, and the mixture of contradictory feelings, such as relief and guilt, sometimes felt confusing as well. This discomfort and confusion made the task of saying goodbye difficult. For those staff who prepared their clients, the process of recognising their clients' and their own feelings, and talking about the ending with them, was emotionally painful. For other staff, the feelings aroused by the ending of the relationship may have been so uncomfortable that they left little or no time to talk about it with their clients.

As we have already noted, the high level of dependency of adults with learning disabilities (particularly those in residential care) can be uncomfortable for staff. Keyworkers who were acutely aware of their clients' physical and emotional dependency often worried about whether the next keyworker would be able to recognise and meet the clients' needs. As one staff member expressed it, *I worried that the next person to step into my shoes would not be so patient.* In this way, the clients' dependency may have contributed to a sense of indispensability in the staff – that is, a feeling that no one else would be able look after the client as well as they could. Siebold (1991) suggests that this feeling of indispensability is a common counter-transference reaction: the staff sense their clients' needs to hold on to the relationship, and therefore the staff find it hard to let go themselves. However, these feelings of indispensability are also understandable in the context of the close, personal relationships that had often developed between staff and clients. Every relationship is unique and cannot simply be replaced by another. As clients and staff often told us, they appreciated each other's unique, personal characteristics. Thus, letting go of the relationship is not easy for either, and worries about what the next relationship will be like are only natural.

In view of the painful feelings aroused by endings, it is not surprising that some staff seemed to deny, or minimise, the impact of their departure on clients. Sometimes, of course, a client may not miss a keyworker, particularly if they have not got on well together; at other times, it may be hard for keyworkers to recognise clients' non-verbal expressions of grief, as we have noted earlier. However, striking inconsistencies in some of the staff's accounts suggested that it was hard to tolerate the clients' feelings of loss. For example, one keyworker talked about the importance of his relationship with a particular client, yet moments later in the interview he asserted that the client would not miss him. Similarly, other keyworkers alternated between recognising their clients' grief and questioning whether clients could really have emotional reactions. These fluctuations between awareness and denial of the impact of loss seem to reflect how uncomfortable it can be for staff to think about the endings of staff–client relationships.

Rosenberg (1990) suggests that staff working with disabled clients have a natural tendency to avoid thinking about emotionally painful issues related to disability. The reality of the client's long-term dependency is perhaps too painful for everyone concerned and may lead to the care worker's avoidance and denial of the client's feelings of grief. Terry (1997), in his sensitive and thoughtful work about caring for older adults with disabilities, also points out that it can be difficult for carers to think about the meaning of clients' difficult behaviours because of the 'unbearable feelings' underlying such behaviours. In the case of staff departures, it may be uncomfortable for carers to think about clients' profound distress and unhappiness, which may only be expressed through their behaviour. Terry urges staff to think about and understand difficult behaviours as communications, rather than attributing them, as is commonly done, to organic causes or personality problems.

Perhaps as another way of avoiding thinking about clients' feelings of loss, many staff tended to minimise the importance of their relationships with their clients. A common feeling was that anyone could step in as keyworker; as one staff member put it, *Someone else could fill your shoes very easily.* Several keyworkers suggested that it was the activities and time spent together, rather than themselves as individuals, that clients would miss. This sense of being dispensable, or easily replaced, contrasts with the feeling of indispensability also expressed by staff (noted above). Some staff seemed to fluctuate between these opposite poles, at times recognising their importance to clients and at other times feeling that they really didn't matter at all. These fluctuations (like those related to recognising the impact of loss, discussed above) may indicate the discomfort staff felt when they thought about their potential importance to clients.

The organisational systems in which staff worked may also have contributed to their tendency to minimise their own importance. Menzies' (1970) well-known study of a hospital nursing service sheds some light on this. Menzies proposed that the structure and culture of an organisation can protect its members from uncomfortable feelings, such as anxiety, guilt or uncertainty. Such aspects of the organisation are referred to as 'socially structured defence mechanisms'. In the case of hospital nursing, certain aspects of the system protected nurses from the uncomfortable feelings aroused by the

person-to-person relationship between nurse and
patient. For example, the system depersonalised both
nurse and patient: patients were referred to by bed
numbers or disease, rather than by name, and nurses
were viewed as an agglomeration of skills, rather than as
individuals. This idea of a 'social defence system' can be
applied to the context of residential care. The feelings
expressed by keyworkers that they were interchangeable,
and mattered only in terms of the tasks and activities
they carried out, may have reflected the culture of the
organisations in which they worked. As in the nursing
system observed by Menzies, the structure and culture
of residential care systems may promote a sense of
depersonalisation, which protects staff from the painful
feelings evoked by their contacts with clients. This sense
of depersonalisation, however, makes it hard for staff to
accurately appraise the role they play in clients' lives.

The self-devaluation of staff – the feeling that they did
not matter – may also have reflected their experience of
not being valued by others. Many staff referred to the
lack of support or recognition from managers. Like the
clients, they were sometimes unthinkingly passed
around the service, without regard to their own feelings
or recognition of their contribution to the service.
Sometimes keyworkers had to rely on the reports of
other staff to convince themselves that they did matter:
they began to realise how important they were to clients
only after they had left and former colleagues told them
of their clients' reactions.

So far, we have discussed why it might be difficult for
staff to think about their clients' – and their own –
feelings about the ending of the keyworker relationship.
However, there is another, related issue: that of talking
about the ending with the client. Even when staff are
aware of the feelings evoked by separation and loss, it
can be hard to raise the issue of ending and allow clients
to express their feelings. As we have seen, staff in our

study sometimes avoided, or put off, telling their clients they were leaving, allowing little time for any discussion. One common reason for this avoidance was that staff wanted to protect their clients. That is, they anticipated how upsetting the news of departure would be, and wanted to spare the client from painful feelings. Rosenberg (1990) suggests that both helper and client avoid confronting topics that generate emotional pain; in this way, they 'conspire' together to avoid talking about important but uncomfortable issues.

Some staff avoided discussing their departure with clients for a more practical reason: they felt unsure about the 'right' way of telling them. Staff working with more disabled clients felt particularly uncertain about how much they would be able to understand and how much time and preparation were needed. These are difficult questions, to which there are no 'right' answers. Clearly clients' cognitive abilities need to be taken into account when preparing them for separation, or for any type of change. For some clients, concepts like time and the future may not make sense and distinctions between reality and fantasy may be hard to make (Barrett and Jones, 1996). Keyworkers were frequently left to struggle with these issues on their own, with little guidance or help from supervisors or managers.

In summary, saying goodbye to clients can be difficult for a complex range of reasons. The dependency of people with learning disabilities on care staff is a painful reality which makes saying goodbye particularly hard. Some staff avoided preparing their clients, not because of malevolence or unkindness, but rather because the feelings brought up by endings were so uncomfortable. Staff sometimes minimised their importance to clients or denied that their departure would have any significant impact, often despite evidence to the contrary. These tendencies to downplay staff's roles and clients' feelings can be understood as defence mechanisms, which were mobilised not only by individuals, but collectively by the service. Although the inclination of staff to protect clients (and themselves) from emotional pain is natural, ultimately it may impede clients' adjustment.

The Importance of Saying Goodbye

The anxieties and pain which accompany separations are rarely faced, yet how these experiences are dealt with is of great importance in determining what of the past can be retained and used creatively in the present and the future. (Salzberger-Wittenberg, 1983, p. 139)

Preparing clients for the endings of keyworker relationships is a first step in facilitating a process of adaptive grieving. As we noted in Chapter 2, the importance of such preparation has long been recognised in the area of psychotherapy (for example, Weiner, 1975). Although there are important differences between psychotherapy and residential care work, in both situations the ending of a close relationship between client and helper can arouse strong feelings, which are akin to those aroused by bereavement. By preparing the client for the separation – which includes providing opportunities for feelings to be expressed and made sense of – helpers can assist clients in the process of mourning. Even when clients and staff are likely to see each other after the keyworker relationship has ended (which frequently occurs in residential care), assistance with mourning is still needed: their relationship will no longer be the same and, as Zinkin (1994) puts it, '[S]omething is indeed lost forever' (p. 20).

Studies of how adults with learning disabilities respond to bereavement indicate how important it is for staff to help clients adjust to loss. Often carers do not recognise clients' grief reactions or respond in a way that facilitates the expression of clients' feelings. For example, they may avoid addressing the issue of loss out of a natural desire to spare the client emotional upset (Seltzer, 1985). Yet the failure to recognise or respond sensitively to clients' feelings is likely to inhibit the grief process and lead to prolonged emotional turmoil and persistent behavioural difficulties (Oswin, 1981, 1991; Ghazziudin, 1988; Harper and Wadsworth, 1993). As Oswin has suggested, many of the problems experienced by people with learning disabilities – including problems such as prolonged or complicated bereavement reactions – arise because they are treated differently from the 'normal' population. The attitude that 'they do not have the same feelings as the rest of us' (Oswin, 1991, p. 26) can thus get in the way of helping clients adjust to the departures of keyworkers.

Saying goodbye – that is, talking with clients about the process of ending and helping them to understand their feelings – is crucial if clients are to develop new relationships in the future. As Rosenberg (1990) points out, we all must grieve for lost relationships, 'or eventually we will lose our capacity to start and maintain new ones' (p. 76). This is true for clients as well as for staff. Like clients, care staff often feel a sense of loss when their relationships end; unless these feelings are recognised it can be hard to begin working with new clients. However, the process of grieving is even more important for people with learning disabilities, who may be sensitised to loss because of multiple losses in the past. Clients' histories may thus make staff departures particularly painful, leading them to feel wary of forming new emotional attachments. Sensitively planned endings, therefore, are essential in order for clients to continue to be able to trust and become close to others.

Finally, facing the difficult issues of endings can ultimately empower clients. The emotional pain of separation can, of course, never be eliminated. But preparation and support can enable clients to adjust to loss and develop skills for coping with future losses. If clients are allowed to take a more active part in the process of change, they may be able to feel a greater sense of control over their lives.

CHAPTER 9

Saying Goodbye: Recommendations for Services

What lessons can we learn from the stories of separation told by clients and staff in this book? How can their experiences be used to improve the care that is provided to adults with learning disabilities? In this chapter, we suggest some ways of planning and preparing for the endings of staff–client relationships. Our central message is that recognising the needs and feelings of clients, as well as those of care staff, can reduce the painfulness and disruption of endings.

Our recommendations draw principally on what clients and care staff in our study told us. Discussions with staff teams and colleagues working in the field, as well as the theoretical literature, have also contributed to our thinking on how best to manage endings. We present our recommendations in two parts. First we address some key aspects of the ending process: telling the client, recognising the client's feelings, recognising one's own (the keyworker's) feelings, and making plans for the client's future care. Then we raise some broader issues for services to consider: the importance of thinking about the nature of the keyworking relationship, expanding clients' social networks, and providing support, supervision and training for staff.

Whilst some of our recommendations pertain to things that individual staff members can do, we strongly believe that the wider systems in which staff work must also change. Individual staff members work not in isolation, but within complex settings which influence how they interact with their clients. Without support and training, and without continued discussion about what the work is all about, care staff will struggle to carry out the demanding responsibilities of their jobs. Staff teams themselves must be 'cared for' in order to enable them to provide the best care possible to their clients.

KEY ASPECTS OF THE ENDING PROCESS

Telling the Client

Perhaps the most important lesson we can learn from clients themselves is that, however painful it may feel for staff and however strong the wish to protect clients, it is crucial that staff talk to clients about the endings of their relationships. Clients need to be given time to process the news about staff departure and to be given the opportunity to identify and express their feelings about it. Helping clients to anticipate and plan for endings, and facilitating the grieving process, can significantly reduce the impact of loss (Siebold, 1991).

Keyworkers may have various reasons for not telling, or for delaying telling, clients that they are leaving. In our study, keyworkers often felt worried and guilty about what impact their departure would have on clients; consequently they postponed or avoided talking about it. Understandably, keyworkers wanted to protect their clients from feeling upset. (Also, understandably, the keyworkers did not want to talk about something that they themselves found upsetting.) Sometimes they felt that they did not know how to tell their clients: without support and supervision, they were uncertain about the best ways of preparing their clients for change. In other cases, keyworkers postponed telling or allowed little time for discussion because they thought their departure would have little impact on their clients. Delays in, or avoidance of, talking about leaving were usually well-intentioned: keyworkers were trying to do the best for their clients, but found the situation difficult.

Clients need honest discussion, careful planning and often lengthy preparation for any major change in their life – the departure of a keyworker being one such change. Not telling the facts may lead to misunder- standings or fantasies about why staff are leaving. For example, clients may wonder whether they have done something terrible to cause their keyworker to leave, or whether they could have done something to make them stay longer. Staff may need to check out the client's understanding of the reasons for their departure, and remind the client of what is happening and why. Gentle reminders can be given, using visual aids such as calen- dars or picture stories, and taking into account how much time is needed for processing the information.

Barrett and Jones (1996) remind us that abstract concepts such as time and the future may not make sense for some clients. It is therefore important to take on board each client's cognitive abilities. The appropriate length of time for preparation will depend on the needs of individual clients. Whilst we have emphasised above the importance of lengthy planning, too long a period of saying goodbye can also be excruciating (for both clients and staff). The issue of timing is a difficult one, with no clear-cut answers. Keyworkers should not be left on their own to struggle with decisions about when and how to tell clients; discussion with, and support from, more experienced colleagues or managers is crucial.

Separations from staff, over which residents have no control, may contribute to the sense of powerlessness and 'learned helplessness' that people with learning disabilities already experience in many aspects of their lives. Staff movement and change is, unfortunately, a reality in the lives of these clients. However, the sense of powerlessness can be reduced if clients are included in discussions and plans concerning their future care.

Separations that occur with little or no warning can only exacerbate feelings of powerlessness; dialogue with residents can enable them to take a more active part in the process of transition.

Staff who are faced with the difficult task of telling their clients that they are leaving might take heed of the words of Jim, a client in our study who clearly articulated the preparation he wanted (see Chapter 5):

> It [discussion with the keyworker] would have had to be on our own ... I wanted privacy on our own ... It would help to have lots of time, to explain why they were leaving and where they were going to, and whether I would be seeing them again.

We think Jim's sentiments reflect those of many residents. Talking together about the ending of the keyworker relationship – and ensuring that there is appropriate time and space to do this – are essential for easing the process of change.

Recognising the Client's Feelings

For all of us, the endings of important personal relationships can be painful. We feel sad and bereft (and sometimes angry and abandoned) when a close friend moves away, when a family member dies, or when we move on in school leaving a much-loved teacher behind. For clients in residential settings, separation from a keyworker can arouse similar feelings.

As we have discussed earlier (see Chapters 4 and 8), keyworkers often play an intimate and central role in residents' lives. They do not simply provide a practical service; because of the nature of the work, they usually develop personal relationships which are highly valued by the client.

Yet we have also seen (in Chapters 7 and 8) how diffi-cult it can be for keyworkers to recognise their importance to clients, and consequently to recognise clients' feelings about separation. Care staff may devalue their own role in clients' lives, perhaps partly because the staff themselves are not valued within the services where they work. For keyworkers who do recog-nise the importance of their role, it can be hard to tolerate the responsibility and guilt of leaving. This in turn may make it difficult to acknowledge or attend to the client's feelings of loss.

The repeated losses that many people with learning disabilities have experienced in their lives can make the ending process particularly complicated. A keyworker's departure is likely to trigger a client's memories of previous losses. The impact of the keyworker's depar-ture consequently may be magnified, and the client's feelings may appear to be out of proportion to the immediate situation. Conversely, clients may appear to have no emotional reaction because they have become accustomed or 'numbed' to repeated losses: the feelings are there, but they are too painful to express. Clients' histories thus provide an important context for making sense of how they might feel when keyworkers leave.

Understanding clients' feelings about separation is a central task for keyworkers who are leaving. This requires empathy, which psychologists define as the process of entering into another person's world, or 'stepping into the other person's shoes'. Empathy is a key aspect of all 'helping' relationships, that is, where one person is providing psychological or emotional help to another (Rogers, 1961, 1973). On the surface, empathy seems easy, yet it can be extraordinarily diffi-cult to put one's own feelings aside and try to understand another person's experience from his or her point of view. This is even more difficult when working with people with learning disabilities, who may not be able to express their feelings clearly in words.

In addition to trying to understand clients' feelings, keyworkers face the task of helping their clients to express and process those feelings. A range of factors can make the process of grieving particularly difficult for adults with learning disabilities: limitations in verbal communication and expression, concrete thought, a confused concept of time, acquiescence and a tendency to adopt a smiling persona, life-long dependency needs, repeated experiences of loss, and a lack of peer relationships. It is important to remember that clients often express their feelings indirectly through their behaviours; difficult or withdrawn behaviour is often an important signal about a client's emotional state. For clients who have severe and profound disabilities, relying on words for communication of feelings and events usually will not suffice. Staff may need to develop alternative ways of communicating, for example using visual aids (here staff can benefit from the advice of speech and language therapy colleagues) or creative media such as art and drama therapy.

Keyworkers need support and supervision in order to recognise and respond appropriately to their clients' feelings. We return to this issue later in this chapter, but we want to make two brief suggestions here. First, keyworkers could be encouraged to draw on their previous observations of how clients have responded to the departure of other staff, particularly those the client had a close relationship with. Several staff in our study told us how they had learned from such experiences. Sometimes it is easier for us to recognise clients' emotional responses when we ourselves are not personally involved. So, reflecting on what we have observed of other clients' and other keyworkers' experiences might be particularly helpful in anticipating what our own clients might need.

Second, it is crucial that staff be given the space to think about, and respond to, their clients' emotional needs. An overload of paperwork and an emphasis on procedures has become part of the fabric of residential work, making it difficult for staff to find time to reflect about what their clients (or the staff themselves) may be feeling. Clearly, services need to create a different kind of culture which recognises the importance of clients' feelings – as well as keyworkers' feelings, a point we now turn to.

Recognising One's Own (the Keyworker's) Feelings

Why consider keyworkers' feelings when we are discussing how to prepare clients for separation? There are two crucial reasons. First, keyworkers' own feelings inevitably enter into the process of saying goodbye. Our own feelings can sometimes get in the way of recognising, and responding to, our clients' feelings. Second, recognising one's own feelings about leaving – and having these feelings acknowledged by supervisors or managers – is critical to keyworkers' own well-being. Endings can be painful and complicated for keyworkers themselves; a lack of emotional support in this situation may adversely affect how keyworkers feel about themselves and their ability to carry out their jobs.

The intense relationships that clients develop with keyworkers in residential settings can lead to complex feelings. As we have seen, keyworkers often feel overwhelmed by the intimacy of the relationship and the dependency of the client. They may feel confused about what the relationship means to them (as well as to their clients). Furthermore, they are often unprepared for the closeness that develops. The nature of the work is not always made clear at the outset, and without training or supervision, care staff may not anticipate their own, or their clients', feelings about their work together.

Care staff may experience a range of feelings when leaving their clients. They may feel relieved to be escaping from a difficult and demanding job, or they may feel excited about the promotion to a new position. They may feel guilty about 'abandoning' a resident and worried that the next keyworker will not be able to meet the resident's needs; sometimes they feel they are the only one who can truly understand the client. Or they may feel that they really don't matter to the client and that all keyworkers are interchangeable. Leaving may stir up keyworkers' own memories of past separations or endings (as it does for clients), and can thus raise uncomfortable feelings about loss for the keyworkers themselves.

It is difficult to pay attention to clients' feelings if we don't understand, and pay attention to, our own feelings. As we noted earlier, all helping relationships involve empathy. But in order to see the world from the client's point of view, the helper has to be able to first recognise her own feelings and set them aside. Helping often breaks down when the helper has difficulty doing this. For example, we have seen in earlier chapters how common it is for keyworkers to feel overwhelmed by a client's dependency; consequently they may feel vastly relieved that the relationship is ending and eager to leave as soon as possible. These feelings can make it difficult for the keyworker to think about the client's experience – which is likely to include a sense of abandonment, in contrast to the keyworker's sense of relief. Without the opportunity to talk about and think through their own feelings with more experienced colleagues or supervisors, how can we expect care staff to respond sensitively to the feelings of their clients?

Planning for the Client's Future Care

Many keyworkers in our study were anxious about what would happen to their clients after they left. Who would be the next keyworker? Would the new keyworker be able to respond to the client's needs? Would the client have setbacks because of the lack of continuity? Similarly, clients were also anxious about what would happen. Who was going to look after them, and would it be someone they liked? Would they be allowed to keep in touch with their previous keyworker?

Clearly, planning for the client's future care is an important part of the process of leaving. In our study we found that handover plans were carefully arranged in some instances, but in others the staff and clients were unaware of what, or whether, plans were in place.

Some services use an effective model of handover in which the new keyworker 'shadows' the old keyworker for a period of time before the old keyworker leaves. This helps the new staff member to get to know the client (for example, her likes and dislikes, special needs, important people in her life, and so on), and consequently to feel confident about taking over as keyworker; it also gives the client time to get used to the new staff member. Keyworkers in our study who had experienced such a handover reported that it was helpful both for themselves and for their clients. Unfortunately, it may not always be possible to have an overlap of care because of limitations on resources (for example, a new staff member may not start until after the previous postholder leaves).

Even when it is not possible to provide an overlap of care, there are ways of easing the transition for the client. For example, telling clients, in advance, the name of their new keyworker (or their temporary keyworker, if new staff have not yet been appointed), may provide some reassurance that they will be looked after. This

may seem an obvious and simple point, but our interviews with clients and staff suggest that it can be
overlooked. Sometimes keyworkers may wish to
maintain informal contact with their clients after
leaving, which can help to ease the process of transition
(Clegg and Lansdall-Welfare, 1995). However, it may
be tempting for staff to promise future contact as a way
of softening the blow of separation, when in fact future
contact is unlikely. Although well-intentioned, such
false promises are likely to lead to even more disappointment than a clean break. Therefore, it is vital that
keyworkers are realistic about the likelihood of future
contact and inform the client accordingly, even if this
may be difficult.

The endings of staff–client relationships may involve
feelings of loss, but they also provide opportunities for
new beginnings. Fredman and Dalal (1998), who have
written about endings in the context of family therapy,
suggest that ideas of loss have dominated how we think
about endings in a therapeutic context. As an alternative, they suggest that we think about endings as
transitions. For example, the final sessions of therapy
provide an opportunity for the client and therapist to
review the therapy and the changes which the client has
made, and to consider how these changes can be carried
forward. In this way client and therapist work together
to address how the client might move on.

This framework for thinking about endings as transitions can be usefully applied to staff–client relationships
in residential settings. Endings can provide an opportunity for keyworkers and clients to reflect together on
what has happened during the course of their work.
They might talk about changes in the client's life, new
skills that she has developed, what she has liked and not
liked about working with the keyworker, and what she
would like more of in the future. This type of review can
help clients to see some continuity in their lives. It is not

intended to replace opportunities for expressing sadness and loss: clearly these feelings must be heard. But looking to the future, thinking about new beginnings and saying hello to new carers are important parts of the process of saying goodbye.

BROADER ISSUES FOR SERVICES TO ADDRESS

What it Means to be a Keyworker

The care staff in our study often felt confused about their roles. Initially keyworkers may view their job as simply providing a service – that is, assisting with the client's physical care and making practical arrangements. Over time, however, what began as a straightforward job can become a complex, personal relationship. A keyworker may be surprised at how involved she becomes in the client's life and how attached they feel to each other.

Many keyworkers in our study expressed a dilemma about how close they should become to their clients. Is it acceptable (and manageable) to become emotionally involved? Or should keyworkers maintain a 'professional' distance and simply carry out the practical tasks required? One of the difficulties with becoming emotionally involved is that the relationship will eventually end: staff often told us they felt guilty about becoming close to clients and then leaving them. Yet staff also felt that their personal relationships with clients were almost an inevitable part of being a keyworker: how could they remain distant when their role encompassed being the client's companion and friend?

Like all of us, people with learning disabilities have a need for close relationships. We strive for intimacy and companionship – to feel known by another, to know another, and to share aspects of our lives with others. Often services for adults with learning disabilities do not seem to recognise this need. Partly as a result of this, the staff member can become one of the few (or only) people with whom a client has a close relationship. Unless clients can be helped to develop broader social networks (a point we address in more detail later), services may unwittingly increase clients' emotional dependence on staff.

The close relationship that can develop between keyworker and client is problematic in at least two ways. First, it is asymmetrical, or unequal. Discrepancies exist between client and keyworker in choice, control and power: the client usually has little say about important aspects of the relationship, for example, when and how often they spend time together and when it will end. Second, the relationship has different meanings for client and keyworker. For keyworkers, it is part of a job and one of many other relationships (both within and outside of the work setting). For clients it is central to their lives: what is a work setting to the keyworker is home for the client, and the keyworker can be a helper, companion, friend and family member all rolled into one.

We would not want readers to conclude that they should keep their distance from clients. Working as a carer is about much more than delivering a 'service'. Attending to clients' physical and practical needs is only one part of the job; responding to their emotional needs is at least as important. We believe that any work with clients (especially in residential care) inevitably involves developing some kind of personal relationship. The nature of the relationship will vary, depending on many factors; some clients and keyworkers will get on well and become quite attached, while others will not. Whatever the relationship, both people involved will have feelings about each other. It is crucial that staff pay attention to these feelings and are aware of what the relationship means to each. With awareness, staff are less likely to feel overwhelmed by clients' emotional dependency and more likely to respond appropriately.

A central task for managers of services is to ensure that staff teams have a forum for thinking about the nature of their work. Care staff sometimes start their jobs with only a vague idea about what the work entails, only to find themselves in the deep end a few weeks or months later. Our study suggests that even more experienced staff often have little opportunity to discuss how they view their roles and the difficulties they encounter. There may be no absolute answers to some of the dilemmas that care work raises, such as that of emotional closeness. Managers may shy away from discussing these issues precisely because clear-cut answers do not exist. We would argue that providing staff with the opportunity to explore what the work means, and to grapple with the dilemmas, is necessary in order for them to carry out their work effectively.

Another issue for staff teams to think about is whether there are ways of reducing the intensity of the keyworker relationship. As we have seen in earlier chapters, staff can feel overwhelmed by their clients' emotional dependency and clients can feel overwhelmed when an all-important keyworker leaves. Again, we are not suggesting that the solution is to avoid close relationships. Rather, the task is for services to review how they work and what they are aiming to do: this might include considering how to prevent an over-reliance on individual carers and how to promote greater independence.

Some staff teams deal with this issue by addressing how the keyworker's role is structured and negotiated with the client. For example, clients can be encouraged to approach other staff who are on duty, rather than relying solely on the keyworker. Keyworking sessions can be set up so that the client knows there are specific times when she can talk about her day, her worries or plans; this can provide 'boundaries' for both client and keyworker. Some teams have a policy of regularly rotating keyworkers, in order to prevent too much closeness or dependency from developing. There can, however, be problems with this if clients feel that a staff member they get on well with is no longer available to them in the same way. Another approach is for two staff members to act as co-keyworkers, sharing the responsibilities of the role. Clearly, keyworking arrangements should be tailored to individual clients' needs, and clients them-selves should be included as much as possible in the process of making such arrangements.

Promoting clients' independence is a larger and more complex issue for services to address. Brechin and Swain (1989) point to care staff's capacity for 'enabling the client'. If staff see their work as encouraging clients' own abilities and responsibilities, rather than doing things for them, then clients may be able to develop a sense of control over their own lives and to find their own voices in making decisions. The keyworker's rela-tionship with her client can also provide a jumping-off point for new relationships. Experiencing a meaningful and satisfying relationship with a keyworker can help a client feel more confident about developing relation-ships with others. The importance of relationships with others is an issue we turn to next.

Expanding Clients' Social Networks

As we have seen, care staff often fill in for other rela-tionships which are absent in clients' lives. A keyworker may come to be experienced as a friend or family member because the client has no friends or family available. Dependency on staff is sometimes unwittingly reinforced by services which do not encourage clients to rely on, or develop friendships with, each other. Clients may consequently come to feel that relationships with other adults with learning disabilities are not valued.

Clients need a broader social network for two impor-tant reasons. The most obvious (but often forgotten) reason is that friendships are crucial for clients' well-being. Social relationships are important for all of us, and have been shown to benefit our physical and psychological health (House et al., 1988). Also, if clients have relationships with others, then separations from keyworkers may have less of an impact. For example, close contact with family members may reduce the intensity of, or balance out, the relationship with the keyworker; consequently the keyworker's departure may not be experienced as such a painful loss.

Firth and Rapley (1990) argue that care staff have a critical role to play in creating opportunities for people with learning disabilities to develop relationships with others. Acting as 'enablers', staff can support clients in important tasks such as getting to know the neighbourhood and the local resources. Firth and Rapley recommend that staff and clients together construct a 'relationship map' to help explore current relationships and think about developing new acquaintances. It is crucial, however, that the wishes of the clients, rather than the staff, are respected: clients themselves will have preferences about who they want to spend time with.

The 'circle of support' concept (Whittaker and McIntosh, 2000), which has become popular in the field of disability, also suggests ways of widening the social networks of clients living in the community. Selected groups of people are invited to befriend adults with learning disabilities and to support them in developing relationships. Advocates, befrienders, parents, neighbours and peers at college can all make important contributions. This approach to expanding clients' social worlds and enhancing their social skills seems a useful way forward.

Staff can also play an important part in helping clients keep up existing friendships. One task for keyworkers might be to think about what conditions would make it easier for clients to get together with acquaintances, friends or partners. For example, privacy – sometimes difficult to find in residential settings – may be needed in order to develop and maintain close relationships. When clients are moved to a new home, change day centres or leave college, they may need support and encouragement to keep in touch with friends and acquaintances left behind. Sadly, without such support, many clients lost important peer relationships after the closure of long-stay hospitals.

Finally, care staff (and other professionals) can offer advice and guidance on social or interpersonal skills which may help clients to make and maintain relationships. Unwritten rules of social behaviour which staff take for granted can present difficulties for clients, who often have been denied opportunities for socialising. Staff can, for example, help clients to recognise and communicate feelings – crucial skills for any relationship. The keyworker relationship itself can provide a vehicle for developing social skills: what the client learns or experiences in this relationship (for example, expressing her own needs and recognising the keyworker's needs) can potentially be applied to other relationships.

Support, Supervision and Training for Staff

Most of the care staff we interviewed told us they received little support or help in thinking about the process of saying goodbye. They were left on their own to decide how and when to tell their clients, and to contend with their own feelings of loss, guilt and uncertainty. Furthermore, many staff referred to a more general lack of support and supervision: they had few opportunities to think about and discuss their work with more experienced colleagues or managers. It is not surprising that staff often ended up feeling overwhelmed by their responsibilities and by the feelings which the work aroused. Several staff in our study told us they had previously left residential units (sometimes giving no notice) because they felt so unsupported by the management.

If clients' distress over separations is to be reduced – and if sudden departures and a high turnover of staff are to be prevented – then services must think about supporting and valuing the staff themselves. Clearly, regular supervision, team meetings and informal opportunities for discussion are crucial. This may seem so obvious that it is hardly worth mentioning; yet we know that, in practice, the needs of staff are often overlooked. Work pressures, lack of resources, and a culture which fails to recognise the value of care staff can all contribute to the neglect of staff's needs.

How can keyworkers be supported in the process of saying goodbye to their clients? In our discussion of key aspects of the leaving process, we have referred to areas where staff may need support and supervision. Telling the client about separation, recognising the client's and one's own feelings, and planning for future care are all complex tasks which keyworkers should not be expected to carry out single-handedly. We add here a few further ideas about how supervision and training sessions – which should be an ongoing part of services, and not just brought in at a point of crisis – might address these issues.

First, supervision and training can provide staff teams with a conceptual understanding of how separations affect clients. Psychological models of attachment, loss and grief can help care workers to make sense of their relationships with clients and of the impact of staff departures. We have already mentioned how separations from staff need to be seen in the context of clients' histories: repeated losses and a paucity of close, stable relationships are bound to affect how clients feel when staff leave. As Kauffman (1994) suggests, a conceptual framework for understanding the grieving process can help staff to recognise the importance of preparing clients for separation and providing opportunities for mourning. With a fuller understanding of such issues, staff might find it easier to reflect on the meaning of previous losses for clients (for example, a family bereavement, the closure of a day centre, or a staff departure), how these were handled in the home, and how to help clients cope with future losses.

Second, supervision can help staff to make sense of their own feelings which arise in their work with clients. For example, helping staff to recognise their own feelings of loss – or, as Kauffman (1994) puts it, the 'mutuality of loss' for client and care worker – may help keyworkers respond more sensitively to their clients. Staff may also benefit from an understanding of how their own history of personal relationships, including previous experiences of caring or being cared for, can affect how they feel about their clients. We all, at times, react to people in ways which are carried over from past experiences; being aware of this can help us to respond more appropriately to our clients. The concepts of transference and counter-transference are relevant here, and can be used within psychodynamically-oriented supervision to help staff understand the complex feelings that sometimes emerge in their work.

Third, supervision can help with the practical issues of preparing clients for changes of keyworker. As we have seen, decisions about how, when and where to talk to clients about the ending of a relationship are often left up to individual keyworkers, many of whom feel uncertain about the correct course of action to take. With supervision, staff can think through what sort of preparation each individual client needs. In addition, staff can be encouraged to think about the importance of the leaving process right from the start of their work with clients. Establishing a new keyworking relationship – that is, the process of saying hello to clients – involves learning about clients' histories and getting a sense of their previous relationships with staff and experiences of endings. If, from the start, staff are aware of their potential importance to clients and of the preparation which clients need for change, then they will be better able to anticipate and respond to clients' needs.

Finally, and most importantly, services must ensure that care staff are given time and space to think about their work and to discuss issues which concern them. We were struck by informal comments made by staff in our study about the (unintentional) benefits of participating in the research: for many staff, the process of being interviewed provided a rare opportunity to reflect on the meaning of their separations from clients. Unfortunately, such opportunities seem to be the exception rather than the rule in many settings. Clearly, this situation must be changed if staff are to carry out their jobs effectively.

SUMMARY AND CONCLUSION

In this final chapter we have considered how separations from care staff might be made less painful for clients. We have made several suggestions about what keyworkers themselves can do, as well as what managers and directors of services can do to facilitate the work of individual staff. These recommendations are not intended as an exhaustive list. We hope, rather, that they will provide a starting point for all those involved in caring for people with learning disabilities to think about the process of saying goodbye.

Preparing clients for separation and change is crucial. This is an issue which must be addressed not only by keyworkers in residential settings, but also by daycare staff, college tutors, respite workers and clinicians. We are all repeatedly involved in making and breaking relationships with clients as part of our work. An understanding of the psychological impact of separation and loss can help us appreciate the importance of planned endings.

It is crucial that care staff are allowed and encouraged to think about their relationships with clients. All too often, services seem to offer few opportunities for staff to reflect on their work. Clearly, changes must be made at a service level in order to instil a culture which values the clients, as well as the care staff. If the needs and feelings of clients and staff are recognised, then the process of saying goodbye is likely to be made easier for all concerned.

Interview Schedule for Residents

Introduction: Getting to Know the Resident

The aim of this introductory section was to get to know the resident – for example, how she spent her time and what sort of relationships she had with others in the house. This section also included some questions about the resident's current and previous keyworkers. (Note: The interview began with a reminder about the purpose and procedure of the interview, which had been explained at a prior meeting with the resident and her keyworker.)

What have you been doing today?

How do you like to spend your time?

What do you normally do during the week?

Who else lives with you in the house? Who do you spend time with?

Who is your keyworker at the moment?

When did s/he start being your keyworker?

Have you had other keyworkers?

Relationship with the Keyworker

In this section the resident was asked to recall a particular keyworker who had left. The aim was to find out about the resident's view of the role of the keyworker:

the kinds of things they did together and what their relationship was like.

Can you remember a particular keyworker who used to work with you and has now left?

What do you remember about that keyworker?

What kinds of things did you do together?

What did you especially like about your keyworker? Was there anything you didn't like?

What made him/her different for you from the other staff in the house?

Did s/he know you [or understand you] well? In what way?

Saying Goodbye

This section focused on what the resident recalled about the process of separation from the keyworker. The questions attempted to elicit some of the resident's memories about what had happened and her understanding of why the keyworking relationship had ended.

Can you tell me about when s/he left – what happened?

How did you know s/he was leaving?

Why did s/he leave? Did she have her own reasons? [Prompt if necessary, for example: new job, moving away.] Were there other reasons?

Did you know before s/he left that she was leaving?

Did you say goodbye to each other?

What else do you remember about that time?

The Impact of Ending

The aim here was to find out about how the resident felt when the keyworker left. Prompts (in the form of words or pictures of faces with different expressions) were used where necessary to enable the client to identify or distinguish different feelings.

How did you feel when s/he left? [Prompt if necessary.]

What happens to you when you feel sad/angry? How would someone know if you were upset?

When [past keyworker] left, did you feel it anywhere in your body?

Did you talk to anyone – to your keyworker or to someone else – about your feelings at that time? If not, why?

What would have made it easier to talk to someone?

How do you think your keyworker felt about saying goodbye to you?

Is there anything that could happen that would make saying goodbye easier?

After the Ending

This section focused on what had happened after the keyworker left (for example, whether the resident had seen the keyworker again) and feelings about new keyworkers.

Do you know where [past keyworker] is now?

Are you still in contact with him/her?

Will s/he be coming back ever?

How would you feel if you saw him/her again?

What happened after s/he left – did you get another keyworker?

How did you feel about the new keyworker?

Do you think the keyworker you have now will leave? Do you ever think about it?

Closing the Interview

Thank you very much for letting me talk to you. How has it felt to be interviewed?

Do you have any questions you want to ask me?

What are you going off to do next, now that we've finished?

Interview Schedule for Staff

Background Information

The aim of this section was to get some information about the client whom the participant had identified for the purpose of the study. The participant was asked to think back to a previous keyworking relationship which had ended because s/he had changed jobs or moved on for other reasons. This section also included questions about why the participant had stopped working with the client and his/her experiences of residential care work. (Note: The interview began with a reminder about the purpose and procedures of the study, which had been explained when the staff member agreed to participate.)

Can you tell me a little bit about the client you've decided to talk about – that is, someone who you used to be keyworker for?

How long were you working together?

How long did you work in that particular home?

What made you decide to leave the post?

Can you tell me something about your experiences of residential care work?

The Keyworking Relationship

This section focused on the participant's perceptions of his/her relationship with the client and role as a keyworker.

How would you describe your relationship with that client?

How did you work together?

How would you define your role as a keyworker with that client?

Saying Goodbye

This section focused on the process of ending the keyworking relationship. It asked about how the client was told and how/whether the client was prepared for the ending.

Can you tell me what happened when you left the post?

What actually happened on the day that you left?

How did the client find out that you were leaving?

What went into your thinking process about deciding to tell (or not to tell)? How did you decide when to tell him/her?

What, if any, preparation do you think the client needed? Did you get any guidance about this from a supervisor or manager?

Looking back on it now, do you think you would do anything differently?

The Impact of Ending on the Client

The aim here was to elicit the participant's view of how his/her departure might have affected the client.

What do you think might have been the impact of your departure on the client?

Did you see him/her at all after you left?

If you had/had not told your client that you were leaving, how do you think s/he would have responded?

The Impact of Ending on the Keyworker

The aim here was to elicit the participant's own feelings about the ending of the keyworking relationship.

What were your own feelings around this time?

What kind of support, if any, did you need around leaving? What support did you get?

Have you had any experiences in the past where important relationships have ended?

Closing the Interview

Thank you very much for participating in the study. How has the interview felt for you?

Do you have any questions you want to ask?

What are your plans for the future – do you intend to stay in the field of residential care work?

APPENDIX C

Interview with 'Eve'

(Note: 'I' stands for the interviewer and 'R' stands for the respondent. In this interview, the respondent is a resident called Eve. All names in the interview are pseudonyms.)

I: Well, Eve, perhaps we can start with just a few questions about you. Is that all right?

R: Yes.

I: Great, so how old are you?

R: 29.

I: Really, and when are you 30?

R: Next year.

I: Right, so you've not long been 29 then?

R: No.

I: I see. Eve, can you tell me a little bit about what you like doing with your free time?

R: Spend a bit of time in my bedroom.

I: In your bedroom?

R: Yes.

I: And what do you do in your bedroom?

R: I can see lots of videos.

I: So you like watching videos?

R: Yes.

I: Anything else?

R: Tidy my room.

I: Gosh, yes, I can see looking around this room. And who do you like spending time with in the house, I wonder? Any of the residents here?

R: One of the boys and one of the girls.

I: Right, so two people. And who is your keyworker at the moment, Eve?

R: Well, it used to be Ruth, then Mandy was my keyworker for a little while, and now it's Norah.

I: Now it's Norah. So you've had three keyworkers here?

R: Yes.

I: And before you lived in this house, I was wondering whether you had any keyworkers anywhere else?

R: No.

I: I see, so where were you living before here?

R: With my mum.

I: So it's quite new to you to have a keyworker?

R: Yes.

I: So when I talk to you now, Eve, if I ask you if you can talk a little bit about a keyworker who has left, who would you be thinking about? Someone who you have said goodbye to.

R: Well, there were two left earlier this year, Wendy and Eileen, and another one left about a couple of weeks ago, Andy.

I: And was Andy your keyworker, Eve?

R: No, Tina's.

I: I see. And did you like Andy?

R: Mm.

I: And was it hard to say goodbye?

R: Yes. And we've got another one leaving a week this Saturday, who's Robin's keyworker – because he's on holiday at the moment.

I: Gosh, it sounds like there are a lot of comings and goings at the moment. I wonder how that feels for you, Eve?

R: Bit strange.

I: And do you remember when your own keyworker left too?

R: Yes.

I: Who was that?

R: Ruth. She left before the end of last year.

I: And is she the one who you said you got a postcard from?

R: Yes.

I: Would you like to talk about Ruth and when she left, or would you like to talk about Norah?

R: Norah came up to me one day when she was doing a sleep-in and I didn't even realise until she told me that she was going to be my keyworker.

I: So Norah is your keyworker at the moment?

R: Yes, 'cause Mandy couldn't cope with two of us, I mean me and Hilary, so Mandy's only Hilary's keyworker now.

I: So Mandy is still here and you still see her, but she's not your keyworker any more?

R: Yes.

I: And can you remember how that felt, Eve?

R: A bit embarrassing.

I: That sounds hard. Can you explain in what way, perhaps?

R: When she said she couldn't cope with two of us residents.

I: Right, I understand. So that made you feel a bit embarrassed.

R: Yes.

I: That sounds very hard. [Pause] I'm wondering whether you think that it was because of you that she left, or because she had too much work on?

R: Too much work on, because of two, because she couldn't cope with two clients.

I: I see, so it feels perhaps a bit embarrassing because she is still here, even though she's not your keyworker any more.

R: Yes.

I: And you've mentioned Ruth, was she your keyworker before Mandy?

R: Yes.

I: And did she actually leave the house?

R: Yes.

I: So you don't see her any more.

R: No.

I: Can you remember what happened when she left?

R: Before she left she told me that she was going around the world. And that was last October.

I: And can you remember what she was like? Can you tell me a bit about her?

R: She had short dark hair.

I: And what was she like also as a person?

R: Nice.

I: She was nice. And what kinds of things did you used to do together?

R: Went up town last year, and went to the cinema down here in [town] to see the film *Mission Impossible*, with Tom Cruise.

I: Oh yes – and did you enjoy that?

R: Yeah.

I: So you used to go out with her sometimes?

R: Yes.

I: And what else did you used to do with her?

R: 'Cause most of us went on a day's outing last August Bank Holiday to Chessington.

I: I see. And did Ruth come with you?

R: Yes.

I: So was Ruth your keyworker for a long time?

R: Soon after when I moved in last year.

I: So she was here when you moved in?

R: Yes.

I: And for how long, do you remember?

R: She was there from July till October.

I: July, August, September, October [counting on fingers], so she was here for about four months?

R: Yeah.

I: Right. And you liked Ruth?

R: Yes.

I: And can you think – I mean I don't know, Eve, you might have ideas about this, but what makes a keyworker different from the other staff in the house?

R: Because they've got different personalities.

I: Different personalities?

R: Yes.

I: That's sure to be true. And is there something that makes a keyworker special to you?

R: Yes.

I: It can be difficult to think about, but mainly what kinds of things might you do with a keyworker that you don't do with any other member of staff, perhaps?

R: You get more time to answer the telephone.

I: You get more time to answer the telephone?

R: Yes.

I: I wonder what that means. [Pause] And anything else?

R: No.

I: No. So you were saying that Ruth left because she went round the world, is that right?

R: Yes.

I: And can you remember how you found out she was leaving?

R: Until that very day she told us, Robin found out so all of us got together to buy her a card and a present.

I: I see, so the day that she told you, you got her a card and a present?

R: Yes.

I: And how long after that did she leave?

R: Same time I went on holiday with two of the other keyworkers and Tina.

I: I see. So did you have a little bit of time after she was leaving?

R: Yes.

I: Was it a couple of weeks?

R: No.

I: More than that or less than that?

R: Less.

I: So was it more like a week or a few days or ...

R: Few days.

I: It was a few days. So one of you found out. Did you say Robin found out – or all of you did?

R: All of us.

I: All of you. So she said she was leaving because she was going round the world?

R: Yes.

I: And I wonder if you can remember how you felt when you found out?

R: Upset.

I: In what way?

R: That she wasn't going to be my keyworker for very long.

I: And were you able to tell her, Eve?

R: Mm.

I: You did, and can you remember what she said?

R: No.

I: I was wondering whether you felt anything else apart from upset?

R: No.

I: Did you feel angry?

R: No.

I: Or did you feel worried?

R: Mm.

I: Can you remember what you were worrying about?

R: Cannot remember.

I: Yes, it's difficult to think about these things isn't it? Does it feel all right talking like this, Eve?

R: Yes.

I: Are you sure?

R: Yes.

I: I was wondering, Eve, you know when you were upset, did you feel it anywhere in your body?

R: Mm.

I: Where did you feel it?

R: [Long pause] Can't think.

I: I think it's very hard to think about it and remember.

R: Yes.

I: When you get upset, how do you know, I wonder? Do you feel it in your body?

R: [Nods]

I: Do you know where you feel it then?

R: Feel it in my eyes.

I: Like tears, maybe?

R: Yes.

I: I see, and I think that's how people can see when we're upset sometimes too – when we're crying.

R: Yes.

I: And did you talk to anyone about being upset that Ruth was leaving?

R: Yes.

I: Do you remember who you talked to?

R: Can't remember.

I: So, how does someone know if you are upset sometimes?

R: By telling them.

I: Aha, and who do you normally tell?

R: One of the other staff.

I: Do you? And is it your keyworker or someone else?

R: Anyone.

I: I see. So where is Ruth now, Eve?

R: Last postcard we had from her is from Australia, then New Zealand.

I: Gosh, that is far away, isn't it. Do you know when she's coming back?

R: Don't know.

I: And do you think you'll see her again ever?

R: I don't know when I'll see her again.

I: I see. That sounds really difficult. [Pause] So Ruth left, and then what happened, Eve?

R: Mandy took over.

I: And how long was she your keyworker for?

R: Since before the end of last year, until a few weeks ago.

I: Oh, it was only a few weeks ago. So you may still have lots of feelings about that. Perhaps we can think about those. You talked about being embarrassed.

R: When she told me that Norah was going to take over as my keyworker, 'cause I didn't even know until after when I came back off my holidays.

I: So you didn't know till then?

R: 'Cause Norah did the same thing when she did that in April till August.

I: Norah did the same thing? I wonder what you mean by that, Eve?

R: She went on holiday around the world – Thailand.

I: Oh, Norah did that as well?

R: Yes.

I: Whilst she was your keyworker?

R: Before she was my keyworker.

I: I see. So because she'd been round the world, what did that make you think, Eve?

R: I thought, 'What's going on?'

I: So you felt a bit confused, maybe?

R: Yes.

I: I wonder how you felt about Norah being your new keyworker?

R: I was worrying about that my keyworker was going to change.

I: You thought she was going to change again?

R: Yes.

I: And what made you think that, Eve?

R: Can't think. [Pause] That I was going to lose one keyworker, then getting another one, then getting a new one.

I: Yes, so you did feel worried about things?

R: Yes.

I: And is Norah still your keyworker now?

R: Yes.

I: And do you still feel worried about it?

R: No.

I: How do you think you managed to feel less worried now?

R: [Pause] I think it was about a few weeks ago until Norah told me.

I: So Norah told you, not Mandy?

R: Mandy told me at first, and then Norah told me soon after.

I: Right. So it sounds like it was a bit of a shock to you.

R: Yes.

I: It seems like it's difficult to think and talk about, isn't it, Eve?

R: Yes.

I: And are you all right thinking about it?

R: Yes. [Eve seemed eager and willing to continue.]

I: So you were a bit worried when you started with Norah that perhaps she would leave?

R: No.

I: Were you worried that you might have to change your keyworker again?

R: Yes.

I: And are you still worrying about that?

R: No.

I: What makes you less worried about that, Eve? Can you say?

R: Not worried, no.

I: Do you know if there is something that makes you feel a little bit better about it?

R: You, you get used to it – having someone new.

I: And do you think that makes it easier?

R: Yes.

I: You know you said you felt worried about losing Norah when she started?

R: Yes.

I: Did you tell her?

R: No.

I: Did you tell anyone you were worried?

R: No.

I: But when you do worry about things normally, who do you tell then?

R: The staff.

I: So it was a bit upsetting when Mandy left?

R: Mandy is still here, won't see her until the day after tomorrow when she's sleeping in.

I: Sorry – I was talking about when she stopped being your keyworker, not when she's left. I'm making things very confusing. When you see her now, do you still speak to her?

R: Yes.

I: And does it feel a bit strange speaking to her sometimes?

R: Yes – she's no longer my keyworker.

I: So how is it different now that she is no longer your keyworker?

R: Well, I still get on, but – we're getting some new staff soon.

I: Right, so lots of changes are happening in the house, aren't they?

R: Yes. Before I came here, Mandy had long dark hair, but now she's got short dark hair.

I: Right, so she looks different?

R: Yes.

I: Eve, have you got anything you want to say to me, that I've forgotten?

R: No.

I: That's fine, I've just got one more question. Is that all right?

R: Yes.

I: I wondered how you felt when you got the postcard from Ruth?

R: Happy.

I: Were you? And do you write to her?

R: Don't have the time.

I: It can be hard to find the time can't it? Well, Eve, *EastEnders* is on at the moment – are you waiting to watch it?

R: Yes please.

I: Thank you very much for talking so honestly.

Interview with 'Gill'

(Note: 'I' stands for the interviewer and 'R' stands for the respondent. In this interview, the respondent is a care worker called Gill. All names in the interview are pseudonyms.)

I: Perhaps the best place to start would be for me to ask, first of all, how long you were working in the residential home that you are about to talk about?

R: Five years.

I: Five years. Right, and did you have one particular key client who you are going to think about now?

R: Yes, she was my key client for four out of five years.

I: I see, so four out of the five years, and was that the last four years?

R: Yes, yes.

I: And what was her name?

R: Margaret.

I: Margaret, OK. Can you tell me a little bit about Margaret?

R: Margaret was challenging – very challenging behaviour – but was quite able, able to do quite a lot for herself, but had hours of very disturbed behaviour where she would wreck her room. Something seemed to come over her and she would become very angry, very frustrated. I think Margaret was so intelligent that she realised that she was slightly different from other people and sometimes this used to hit her and she used to become very angry, with herself and with everyone else, with the whole world really. She would become very depressed, very introvert. And fortunately – well, she was in a unit where she's been moved from now, but she was in a unit where she was the only resident with any speech, a lot of speech.

I: Aha.

R: A very articulate lady, very repetitive, but very articulate and the only people she had to speak to were the staff.

I: I see.

R: So she used to get very heavy crushes on the male members of staff, and didn't want anything to do with any of the other clients, would spend a lot of time in her own room. She would come out now and again, was getting better, but she seemed to almost look down on the other clients there.

I: So she was quite attached to the different members of staff.

R: Yes, she used to get very attached to members of staff, and she used to mention members of staff that had left years ago, because Margaret had been in residential care since she was 15 and she's now 32. So yes, very attached to members of staff.

I: So I guess that may have had implications for your relationship, and I wonder …

R: Yes it was, because Margaret would get very close, very close, but she did prefer male members of staff.

I: Aha. And when you say she got very close, did she get very close to you as well?

R: Yes.

I: So you were her keyworker. How would you describe your role in that relationship with Margaret – as her keyworker?

R: Well, really in a way you felt that you had to stand back a bit, because she would get so close to one person that she didn't want any contact with any other member of staff. And if you weren't there she would shout for you.

I: Aha.

R: She would shout your name. I've been back quite a few times to take her out for a meal – spent the evening with her, and as soon as, I didn't see her for about ... [Gill looked sad as she recalled the events] ... My former manager advised me it would be an idea to withdraw for a little while and then go back and visit, to give her time to get used to me going.

I: Do you mean after the time you had left?

R: Yes, after I had left, so I withdrew for about three months, and there was a club that Margaret went to every Wednesday night, and I walked into the club and this lady ran from the other end of the club just shouting my name from one end to another. So you know, it was quite difficult for her. She did used to attach herself. But then, as I say, she did used to shout for members of staff that she had known years ago, years before.

I: Gosh, yes, so she saw you after three months of not having seen you, and then how did she respond? Was she angry or ...?

R: No, no, she just threw herself at me, yes. Now she has since attached herself to another member of staff, so she will.

I: Her keyworker?

R: No it isn't her keyworker, strangely enough, it's another member of staff, yeah, so she will – I think she's been in care for so long that she's learned that people will probably go through her life and leave and then she'll probably see them occasionally, but she won't see them so often.

I: Yes.

R: So I think she has come to the realisation that this is what happens, that there's going to be lots of people going through her life.

I: Perhaps that was in your mind when you actually left? Gosh, four years is a relatively long time to be a keyworker, isn't it?

R: Yes.

I: Can you tell me a little bit about when you left? What actually happened at the time?

R: Well, I actually started telling Margaret about two months before I left, gradually told her. When I first told her she totally ignored me, turned her head the other way, didn't want to understand, didn't want to know really. Apparently this had been her reaction with other people she had become attached to.

I: I see.

R: She would ignore it, turn her head, didn't want to know, changed the subject, stopped talking. As I say, she was very repetitive. She would say where was her duvet constantly. Where were items of clothing, over and over again. And when you started talking about this she would start doing the repetitive speech, switching off, she would totally switch off. So it had to be a long, gradual process of telling her that you were actually leaving. Yeah, so it was, yes, very sad, both for her and for me.

I: Yes, I was going to ask you how it did make you feel, I was wondering.

R: [Laughing nervously] The last day I was very, very sad, yes, very sad to leave.

I: Yes, it must have been really difficult.

R: Well, I took her on several holidays as well, which it, well just talking about it, I don't think it is a good idea to keywork for such a length of time, to be honest. In retrospect I think it's perhaps better to change about every year, different keyworkers, because the relationship does become too strong.

I: Do you think that is the case – and for both sides?

R: Yes. I was about to say that too.

I: That's interesting, because I suppose it probably is quite unusual to have that intensity within a working relationship.

R: Yes, that length of time.

I: Yes, and so you were the person that told Margaret that you were going?

R: Yes, I was.

I: And what do you think was the impact on her during those two months and afterwards? Do you know or have any thoughts?

R: Yes, apparently she became very withdrawn. Her repetitive speech became more, a very articulate lady but when people spoke to her she would start to switch off and start doing the 'Where's my duvet?', and all the repetitive stuff. Then she started coming round and becoming attached to another member of staff.

I: Whilst you were there?

R: No, this was after I left, after I had gone.

I: So when you first told her you were leaving, was it as if she was becoming more disabled in a way?

R: Yes, oh yes, she was going back. She was withdrawing more to her room, just sitting on her bed, listening to her music – whereas she had been coming out a bit more. She seemed very much more off-hand with other clients who she didn't have much to do with anyway, but she became a bit more withdrawn with them as well. But that gradually recovered after I had actually left. While I was still doing shifts, while I was still there, she just sort of switched off and withdrew from me.

I: I see.

R: But once I had actually left ... I had explained to her that I was leaving, that I would come back and visit. I explained that I would come back and visit and I'd take her out for a meal occasionally and things like that. She was very withdrawn from me, yeah.

I: And you said at the beginning that she was quite challenging in her behaviour.

R: She is very challenging, yeah.

I: Did her behaviour then become more challenging?

R: No, no, just more withdrawn.

I: Just more withdrawn, that's interesting isn't it?

R: Yeah, yeah.

I: You said it was difficult at the end. Can you tell me a little bit more about your feelings in those two months and afterwards? It may be quite difficult to think about, perhaps.

R: Yeah, I kept thinking about her, and also being very tempted to sort of visit. If you drove near the home, you'd feel like knocking and saying, 'Can I go in and visit Margaret?' But I was told that it was a good idea to let her have a cooling-off period, of six weeks to two months. But it was very tempting to ring up and say, 'Is it all right to go in and visit Margaret?'

I: Yes, I understand.

R: I mean, I'm only thinking of one person at the moment, but it wasn't only Margaret. There was a guy I keyworked as well, and it was the same sort of thing with him. Not quite as strong as with Margaret. But you were very tempted to pop in. Yes, he was called Tony.

I: Had that also been a long keyworking relationship?

R: Yeah, but Tony was a different character. Tony was, well tough is the wrong word, but he was more adapt-able. He would adapt as soon as someone would move on and switch to the next person. So he didn't take it quite so hard. And he wasn't so able as Margaret, not quite so thinking. He was – as I say, Margaret was so articulate, a kind of thinking lady. She would sit on her bed and think. But Tony was tougher, and he'd switch off from one person to the next person, no problem.

I: So there was a difference between the way they handled the situation?

R: Oh yes, a big difference, yeah. Tony just accepted it as part of life, a way of life. But then again, Tony had a very strong – I think this makes a difference – Tony had a very strong bond with his family.

I: I see.

R: His dad would come every Saturday, take him out all day. He would spend holidays with them, everything. Whereas Margaret didn't see an awful lot of her family, so I think staff became a sort of surrogate family. I'm assuming, I don't know, but I think that might be it. Tony's family were first, so he'd always got them, and staff were just staff.

I: So perhaps what you are saying is that staff were more like Margaret's family?

R: A bit of a surrogate family, yeah.

I: And you said that she's been in residential care since she was 15.

R: A long time, yeah. Whereas Tony was different. Tony didn't come into residential care until he was 21. And he was then in his early thirties, so his family had always been there.

I: And Margaret's family, did they ever visit her?

R: Not very often, no.

I: That sounds an important point, as you say, that the attachment to the client may be especially strong when you are more like a member of her family – Margaret's family.

R: That's right, yeah.

I: I see. I just wondered about, well, you mentioned that your manager had advised you to withdraw gradually.

R: Yes.

I: So, I wanted to ask you a bit about the guidance or support that you had around that process of preparing to leave.

R: A lot. Well, very good, yeah. The manager was very good. I was lucky, he was a very good manager and he supported me through it. I mean you could say it's like a bereavement in a way. For Margaret it was a bereavement and for myself as well, really. I mean you've lost a good friend, haven't you?

I: Yes, yes, and that sounds really hard.

R: Well you haven't lost them, but you're not having so much contact with them.

I: Yes, and bereavement seems to be a very helpful way of describing some aspects of this process.

R: Yes, I think it is a bereavement, yes. Because it is the loss of a friend. You haven't lost them, but then again. You know, when I first saw her at the club afterwards, I was really sort of choked up, and you sort of want to know all about her. Is she going on holiday? Is she doing this? Is she doing that? And you sort of feel, 'Well I could be organising that.' You know, you do feel very [laughs] – as you say, it's a bereavement.

I: Yes, and on both sides as well, it sounds like – as much about how you felt as it was about how she felt.

R: Yes, yes, and of course Margaret had to find somebody else really. Because, as I say, she has since attached herself to another member of staff, and she's now in the process of moving, so then again, it will be new staff and a new place to live, and also for Tony.

I: Aha.

R: Because you see this was an old institutional building, and they are all being moved out, in the community, into small housing. So she'll be in a new setting, new staff, new people, you know, new people altogether. So that's going to be hard, yeah.

I: Yes. I just wondered, you mentioned that she had attached herself to another member of staff. I wonder how that made you feel?

R: A little bit jealous, yes, a little bit jealous. But then again relief, because then you knew she was OK, because she did need that support and somebody to talk to really. Because as I say, she would sit on her bed and just think for hours, and you knew that it was all going round her head, and then she would suddenly wreck her room, for no apparent reason. And we really surmised that it was just the thoughts that were going through her head, and then suddenly she would just go mad – totally wreck everything.

I: This was around the time you were leaving, or in general?

R: This was in general, so as I say, we knew that she was a very sensitive, thinking lady. And she picked up a lot on atmospheres and things around her, so you've got to be more careful with her than – it sounds terrible – but you've got to be more careful with her than, say, Tony or any of the other clients, because, as I say, she felt things a lot more.

I: You felt that she felt things more?

R: Yes, yes.

I: It must have been very difficult. With hindsight, do you think you would have gone through the same process around leaving? You say that perhaps you wouldn't have keyworked for such a long time, which I think is an interesting point.

R: I don't think that is a good idea, no, especially for somebody like Margaret. I think that keyworking, the longest should be a year, and then another keyworker should come in. But I mean it should be handed over properly, you know, also as I was saying, explain what I want beforehand. You know that you are still their friend, that whatever, you are still going to be in the building, but you know, whoever is going to take over the role of being Margaret's advocate. Because a keyworker doesn't necessarily have to be a friend, you know you are their friend, but it doesn't have to be the one that Margaret's attached to, or any other client is attached to, because basically you are their advocate.

I: Yes.

R: So it doesn't have to be somebody that they are totally attached to.

I: But for you it was?

R: It was, yes, it became a relationship.

I: And how did the handover happen?

R: I did the handover.

I: So whilst you were keyworking somebody else was stepping into your place?

R: Yes, and it was somebody that Margaret had known for a long time, which was a good thing, yes. Because I didn't want anyone new. Because my post wasn't filled for about two months anyway, so you didn't really want anybody new stepping in.

I: Yes.

R: So it was a lady that she had known for a long time, which is a good thing. Although strangely enough that wasn't the person that Margaret became attached to. It was another lady who wasn't keyworking at all in the building.

I: I wonder why that was. Do you have any thoughts about that?

R: I don't know, it's strange really. I don't know, unless it was that Margaret was such a deeply thinking lady, intelligent lady that – you don't know – she might have thought, 'I'm not getting attached to a keyworker again.'

I: I see.

R: Because it happened before me, there was another lady that she shouted for that used to keywork Margaret before I came, and she used to shout for her sometimes, or ask for her. She would say 'Where's Sophie, is Sophie coming?' This lady was called Sophie, and she had left sort of five or six years previously.

I: And was that something that happened throughout your time there?

R: Oh yeah, she would ask for people from years ago – you know, people at school, you know that she'd been attached to. She'd ask for – I mean my manager was saying one day, 'If you think of people who've been in residential care since they were 14 or 15 years old, how many people have gone through their lives?'

I: Absolutely.

R: So yeah, and staff turnover in some residential homes is so high that it's devastating really. There were some residents – one particular young lady there who didn't become attached to anybody, she just totally switched off, because she had probably got a tough exterior. She had been in care since she was five, so she had developed this tough exterior, thinking, 'If I get attached to somebody, they're going to up and go.' So she never got attached to anybody, she was just for herself – let's put it that way.

I: Gosh, and that seems to make sense really. And I suppose what you were saying before about Margaret, it sounds like that has almost started with her. She wasn't allowing herself to become as attached to the next keyworker.

R: That's right, yes, because if you count – I mean you're probably going into hundreds, a hundred-plus people who have gone through their lives if they have been in care for some time.

I: Yes. It sounds, Gill, as though you still think a lot about Margaret.

R: Oh yes, well I still see Margaret. I don't go so often, but there is the club that she goes to and I go down to the club, and she's usually there all evening, so I spend the evening with her. It's the [name of club]. I try and go every six weeks – spend the evening, because I know everyone there. We've been on lots of holidays. We went to EuroDisney, you know, we've done lots of things together. So, and it's run by parents, but they do invite people from over the borough who would like to go, so Margaret goes on a weekly basis, yes. So I do try and pop back, but she's not quite so exuberant now.

I: Isn't she?

R: No, she'll come over and sit by me, and she'll talk and she'll talk and she'll talk, but her face lights up. But she's not quite so ... I mean the first time I went there – she's a big lady of about 14 stone, and she nearly knocked me on my back [Laughs briefly]. But now it's calmed down quite a lot, so obviously she feels better in herself.

I: So at the moment you're bank staff aren't you?

R: That's right, yes.

I: So you're not actually keyworking at the moment?

R: I've been on a contract, so I've been temporary keyworking two guys here, but it's not quite the same because it's on a temporary basis.

I: And can you see yourself keyworking again?

R: I will, yes, but I haven't been ready yet, because as I say, with Margaret it was five years and I felt I wanted to go around a bit and get a bit more experience, I didn't want to get to that involvement stage. But now I've been here for about eight months and I'm really sorry to leave. So I will start looking for permanent work.

I: Well, that's really interesting, because in a way what you are saying is that you experienced a similar reaction to Margaret in not wanting to form another relationship so quickly at the end of a long relationship.

R: That's true, yes.

I: Perhaps you didn't want to get so attached to another client, in the same way as she didn't want to have and then lose another keyworker?

R: That's right, yes – I didn't want to get so involved, yes.

I: It sounds as though it was a mutually very important relationship.

R: Oh that's it, yes.

I: Well it's been so interesting finding out a bit about that relationship. Just as a closing question: when you are next a full-time keyworker, apart from what you said about being in a shorter-term keyworking relationship, can you think of any other way that you might do things differently? Or do you think you had a good model of leaving?

R: Well, it's been done very well here [Gill's present place of work], as well, because I was handed over from

the guy, David, who was keyworking these two
gentlemen. One of them was a new client from respite
and he's moving on at the end of the year. I had to go to
all the planning meetings and negotiate with his parents
– that's another thing, negotiation with parents – but it's
all been done very well. They know that I'm leaving and
they know they'll go back to being with David. So
they're going back to somebody that they were with
before – not somebody new. So they're quite happy with
that, it's not quite so traumatic.

I: Well that's good.

R: Yes, well here they have a different system, they do
change over regularly. I think it's every two years here,
they change over.

I: And you think that's a positive thing?

R: Yes I do.

I: Do you think you will stay working in residential care
with adults with learning disabilities in the future?

R: Oh gosh, yes, I enjoy it too much.

I: I can hear that just by talking to you today.

R: Yes.

I: Well, that's been really interesting. Thank you very
much.

R: Well, I hope it's been helpful.

I: It's been really helpful, because you've talked about
lots of different aspects of leaving, both from your
perspective and Margaret's, and also the different
example of Tony.

R: Different people react in different ways – only I can
tell you, it's not keyworking, but a lady – I hope she
doesn't mind me mentioning, I'm sure she doesn't.

Carol, who is my manager now, also worked the same place that I worked. She was managing there, and she was quite attached to a young lady there, Penny, and Penny would go running up to her, you know, really excited. Now she went back to visit and to pick up some paperwork there two weeks, just two weeks after she had left, and she was saying to me the reaction is unbelievable. Penny would always run up to her, put her arms around her you know – really attached. Carol walked in the place, into the room, and Penny looked at her, turned round and walked out of the room, didn't want to know. Wouldn't talk to her, look at her or have anything to do with her whatsoever, so this is the way residents must feel. This woman that's been here all this time, that I like, that she liked very much, she was almost saying 'Blow you, you're not here any more.' Carol said she went back two or three times and Penny would not talk to her, wouldn't have anything to do with her.

I: Really. Well that's interesting, and in a way it's similar to what you were saying about Margaret's withdrawal from you, because she's not with you any more. How does that make you feel?

R: Yes. Well, pleased for Margaret, because then you know she's adjusted and she's happy – well as happy as Margaret will be in her life. But, yes, you do feel a bit strange.

I: Yes, well you've been very much together, haven't you, and suddenly you're not any more – it's very, very difficult. Well that's been so interesting. Thank you.

References

Allen, P., Pahl, J. and Quine, L. (1990). *Care Staff in Transition: The impact on staff of changing services for people with mental handicaps*. London: HMSO.

Arthur, A.R. (1999). 'Emotions and people with learning disability: are clinical psychologists doing enough?' *Clinical Psychology Forum, 132*, 39–43.

Atkinson, D. (1988). 'Research interviews with people with mental handicaps'. *Mental Handicap Research, 1*, 75–90.

Atkinson, D. (1989). *Someone To Turn To: The social worker's role and the role of front line staff in relation to people with mental handicaps*. Kidderminster: British Institute of Mental Handicap Publications.

Bailey, N.M. and Cooper, S.A. (1999). 'Community care for people with learning disabilities using health services following resettlement'. *British Journal of Learning Disabilities, 27*, 64–9.

Bailey, R., Matthews, S. and Leckie, C. (1986). 'Feeling: the way ahead in mental handicap'. *Mental Handicap, 14*, 65–7.

Barker, C., Pistrang, N. and Elliott, R. (1994). *Research Methods in Clinical and Counselling Psychology*. Chichester: John Wiley.

Barrett, H. and Jones, D. (1996). 'The inner life of children with moderate learning difficulties', in V. Varma (ed.), *The Inner Life of Children with Special Needs* (pp. 45–62). London: Whurr Publishers Ltd.

Beail, N. (1989). 'Understanding emotions', in D. Brandon (ed.), *Mutual Respect: Therapeutic approaches to working with people who have learning difficulties*. Surbiton: Good Impressions.

Beail, N. (1995). 'Outcome of psychoanalysis, psychoanalytic and psychodynamic psychotherapy with people with intellectual disabilities: a review'. *Changes*, *13*, 186–91.

Beail, N. (1998). 'Psychoanalytic psychotherapy with men with intellectual disabilities: a preliminary outcome study'. *British Journal of Medical Psychology*, *71*, 1–11.

Bender, M. (1993). 'The unoffered chair: the history of therapeutic disdain towards people with a learning difficulty'. *Clinical Psychology Forum*, *54*, 7–12.

Bicknell, J. (1983). 'The psychopathology of handicap'. *British Journal of Medical Psychology*, *56*, 167–78.

Bowlby, J. (1969). *Attachment and Loss*. Volume 1. *Attachment*. London: Hogarth.

Bowlby, J. (1973). *Attachment and Loss*. Volume 2. *Separation, Anxiety and Anger*. London: Hogarth.

Bowlby, J. (1980). *Attachment and Loss*. Volume 3. *Loss, Sadness and Depression*. London: Hogarth.

Bowlby, J. (1988). *A Secure Base: Clinical applications of attachment theory*. London: Routledge.

Brechin, A. and Swain, J. (1989). 'Creating a "working alliance" with people with learning difficulties', in A. Brechin and J. Walmsley (eds), *Making Connections: Reflecting on the lives and experiences of people with learning difficulties* (pp. 42–53). London: Hodder and Stoughton.

Bretherton, I. (1991). 'Pouring new wine into old bottles: The social self as internal working model', in M.R. Gunnar and L.A. Sroufe (eds), *Self-process and Development* (pp. 1–41). Hillsdale, NJ: Lawrence Erlbaum Associates.

Burgess, R.G. (1984). *In the Field: An introduction to field research*. London: Allen and Unwin.

Chapman, K. and Oakes, P. (1995). 'Asking people with learning disabilities their view on direct psychological interventions'. *Clinical Psychology Forum*, *81*, 28–33.

Chappell, A.L. (1994). 'A question of friendship: community care and the relationships of people with learning difficulties'. *Disability and Society*, *9*, 419–34.

Charmaz, K. (1995). 'Grounded theory', in J.A. Smith, R. Harre and L. Van Langenhove (eds), *Rethinking Methods in Psychology* (pp. 27–49). London: Sage.

220   SAYING GOODBYE

Clegg, J.A. (1993). 'Putting people first: a social construc-
tionist approach to learning disability'. *British Journal of
Clinical Psychology, 32,* 389–406.

Clegg, J.A. and Lansdall-Welfare, R. (1995). 'Attachment and
learning disability: a theoretical review informing three
clinical interventions'. *Journal of Intellectual Disability
Research, 4,* 299–305.

Clegg, J.A., Standen, P.J. and Cromby, J.J. (1991).
'Interactions between adults with profound intellectual
disability and staff'. *Australia and New Zealand Journal of
Developmental Disabilities, 17,* 377–89.

Clegg, J.A., Standen, P.J. and Jones, G. (1996). 'Striking the
balance: a grounded theory analysis of staff perspectives'.
British Journal of Clinical Psychology 35, 249–64.

Craft, A. and Craft, M. (1981). 'Sexuality and mental
handicap: a review'. *British Journal of Psychiatry, 139,*
494–505.

Day, K. (1985). 'Psychiatric disorder in middle-aged, elderly
mentally handicapped'. *British Journal of Psychiatry, 147,*
665–8.

Department of Health (1991). *Health Services for People with
Learning Disabilities (Mental Handicap).* Draft circular.
London: HMSO.

Dozier, M., Cue, K.L. and Barnett, L. (1994). 'Clinicians as
caregivers: role of attachment organization in treatment'.
Journal of Consulting and Clinical Psychology, 62, 793–800.

Dunn, J. (1993). *Young Children's Close Relationships: Beyond
attachment.* London: Sage.

Emerson, P. (1977). 'Covert grief reaction in mentally
retarded clients'. *Mental Retardation, 15,* 46–7.

Felce, D., Repp, A.C., Thomas, M., Ager, A. and Blunden, R.
(1991). 'The relationship of staff:client ratios, interactions,
and residential placement'. *Research in Developmental
Disabilities, 12,* 315–31.

Firth, H. (1986). 'A move to the community: social contact
and behaviour'. Unpublished manuscript, Northumberland
Health Authority District Psychology Service, Morpeth,
England.

Firth, H. and Rapley, M. (1990). *From Acquaintance to
Friendship: Issues for people with learning disabilities.*

Kidderminster: British Institute of Mental Handicap Publications.

Flynn, M.C. (1986). 'Adults who are mentally handicapped as consumers: issues and guidelines for interviewing'. *Journal of Mental Deficiency Research, 30,* 369–77.

Flynn, M.C. (1989*)*. *Independent Living for Adults with Mental Handicap: A place of my own.* London: Cassell.

Frankish, P. (1989). 'Meeting the emotional needs of handicapped people: a psycho-dynamic approach'. *Journal of Mental Deficiency Research, 33,* 407–14.

Fredman, G. and Dalal, C. (1998). 'Ending discourses: implications for relationships and actions in therapy'. *Human Systems: The Journal of Systemic Consultation and Management, 9,* 1–13.

Gallimore, R., Weisner, R.S., Kaufmann, S. and Bernheimer, L.P. (1989). 'The social construction of ecocultural niches'. *American Journal of Mental Retardation, 94,* 216–30.

George, M.J. and Baumeister, A.A. (1981). 'Employee withdrawal and job satisfaction in community residential facilities for mentally retarded persons'. *American Journal of Mental Deficiency 85,* 639–47.

Ghaziuddin, M. (1988). 'Behavioural disorder in the mentally handicapped: the role of life events'. *British Journal of Psychiatry, 152,* 683–6.

Glaser, B.G. and Strauss, A.L. (1967). *The Discovery of Grounded Theory: Strategies for qualitative research.* Chicago, IL: Aldine.

Goldberg, D., Magrill, L., Hale, J., Damaskinidou, K., Paul, J. and Tham, S. (1995). 'Protection and loss: working with learning-disabled adults and their families'. *Journal of Family Therapy, 17,* 263–80.

Harper, D.C. and Wadsworth, J.S. (1993). 'Grief in adults with mental retardation: preliminary findings'. *Research in Developmental Disabilities, 14,* 313–30.

Hastings, R.P. and Remington, B. (1994). 'Staff behaviour and its implications for people with learning disabilities and challenging behaviours'. *British Journal of Clinical Psychology, 33,* 423–38.

House, J.S., Landis, K.R. and Umberson, D. (1988). 'Social relationships and health'. *Science, 241,* 540–5.

James, I.A. (1995). 'Helping people with learning disability to cope with bereavement'. *British Journal of Learning Disabilities, 23,* 74–8.

Kanner, L.A. (1964). *A History of the Care and Study of the Mentally Retarded.* Springfield, IL: Charles C Thomas.

Kauffman, J. (1994). 'Mourning and mental retardation'. *Death Studies, 18,* 257–71.

Kushlick, A., Blunden, R. and Cox, G. (1973). 'A method of rating behaviour characteristics for use in large scale surveys of mental handicap'. *Psychological Medicine, 3,* 466–78.

Landesman-Dwyer, S. and Berkson, G. (1984). 'Friendships and social behaviour', in J. Wortis (ed.), *Mental Retardation and Developmental Disabilities.* Volume 13. London: Plenum Press.

Lanyado, M. (1989). 'United we stand ...?: stress in residential work with disturbed children'. *Maladjustment and Therapeutic Education, 7,* 136–46.

Menzies, I.E.P. (1970). *The Functioning of Social Systems as a Defence Against Anxiety.* London: The Tavistock Institute of Human Relations.

Miles, M.B. and Huberman, A.M. (1994). *Qualitative Data Analysis: An expanded sourcebook* (2nd edn). Thousand Oaks, CA: Sage.

Oswin, M. (1981). *Bereavement and Mentally Handicapped People: Discussion paper.* London: King's Fund.

Oswin, M. (1991). *Am I Allowed to Cry? A study of bereavement amongst people with learning difficulties.* Human Horizon Series.

Parkes, C.M. (1972). *Bereavement: Studies of grief in adult life.* London: Tavistock Publications.

Perske, R. (1972). 'The dignity of risk and the mentally retarded'. *Mental Retardation, 10,* 25–7.

Pidgeon, N. and Henwood, K. (1996). 'Grounded theory: practical implementation', in J.T.E. Richardson (ed.), *Handbook of Qualitative Research Methods for Psychology and the Social Sciences* (pp. 86–101). Leicester: BPS Books.

Powers, B.A. (1992). 'The roles staff play in the social networks of elderly institutionalized people'. *Social Science and Medicine, 34,* 1335–43.

Robson, C. (1993). *Real World Research: A resource for social scientists and practitioner-researchers.* Oxford: Blackwell.

Rogers, C.R. (1961). *On Becoming a Person.* Boston, MA: Houghton Mifflin.

Rogers, C.R. (1973). 'The interpersonal relationship: the core of guidance', in C.R. Rogers and B. Stevens (eds), *Person to Person: The problem of being human* (pp. 89–103). London: Souvenir Press.

Rosenberg, M.L. (1990). 'Disability and the personal-professional connection', in B.Genevau and R.S. Katz (eds), *Countertransference and Older Adults* (pp. 69–79). London: Sage.

Rubino, G., Barker, C., Roth, T. and Fearon, P. (in press). 'Therapist empathy and depth of interpretation in response to potential alliance ruptures: the role of therapist and patient attachment styles'. *Psychotherapy Research.*

Salzberger-Wittenberg, I. (1983). 'Different kinds of endings', in G. Henry, E. Osborne and I. Salzberger-Wittenberg (eds), *The Emotional Experience of Learning and Teaching* (pp. 139–54). London: Routledge.

Seligman, M.E. (1975). *Helplessness: On depression, development and death.* San Francisco, CA: W.H. Freeman.

Seltzer, G.B. (1985). 'Selected psychological processes and aging among older developmentally disabled persons', in M.P. Janicki and H.M. Wisniewski (eds), *Aging and Developmental Disabilities: Issues and approaches* (pp. 222–4). Baltimore, MD: Paul H. Brookes.

Shlien, J.M. (1973). 'A client-centred approach to schizophrenia: first approximation', in C.R. Rogers and B. Stevens (eds), *Person to Person: The problem of being human* (pp. 151–65). London: Souvenir Press.

Siebold, C. (1991). 'Termination: when the therapist leaves'. *Clinical Social Work Journal, 19,* 191–204.

Sigelman, C.K., Budd, E.C., Spanhel, C.L. and Schoenrock, C.J. (1981). 'Asking questions of retarded persons: a comparison of yes–no and either–or formats'. *Applied Research in Mental Retardation, 2,* 347–57.

Sinason, V. (1986) 'Secondary mental handicap and its relation to trauma'. *Psychoanalytic Psychotherapy, 2,* 131–54.

Sinason, V. (1992). *Mental Handicap and the Human Condition: New approaches from the Tavistock.* London: Free Association Books.

Smith, H. and Brown, H. (1989). 'Whose community, whose care?', in A. Brechin and J. Walmsley (eds), *Making Connections: Reflecting on the lives and experiences of people with learning difficulties* (pp. 229–36). London: Hodder and Stoughton.

Strachan, J.G. (1981). 'Reactions to bereavement: a study of a group of mentally handicapped hospital residents'. *Apex, 9,* 20–1.

Strauss, A. and Corbin, J. (1998). *Basics of Qualitative Research: Techniques and procedures for developing grounded theory* (2nd edn). Newbury Park, CA: Sage.

Swain, J. (1989). 'Learned helplessness theory and people with learning difficulties: the psychological price of powerlessness', in A. Brechin and J. Walmsley (eds), *Making Connections: Reflecting on the lives and experiences of people with learning difficulties* (pp. 109–18). London: Hodder and Stoughton.

Swanson, A.J. and Schaefer, C.E. (1988). 'Helping children deal with separation and loss in residential placement', in C.E. Schaefer and A.J. Swanson (eds), *Children in Residential Care: Critical issues in treatment* (pp. 19–20). New York: Van Nostrand Reinhold.

Symington, N. (1981). 'The psychotherapy of a subnormal patient'. *British Journal of Medical Psychology, 54,* 187–99.

Terry, P. (1997). *Counselling the Elderly and their Carers.* London: Macmillan.

Twigg, J. and Atkin. K. (1994). *Carers Perceived: Policy and practice in informal care.* Buckingham: Open University Press.

Wadsworth, J. and Harper, D.C. (1991). 'Grief and bereavement in mental retardation: a need for a new understanding'. *Death Studies, 15,* 101–12.

Wallace, W. (2000). 'National/London learning disability strategy'. Paper presented at the conference of the Psychologists' Special Interest Group in Learning Disabilities, Abergavenny, Wales.

Weiner, I.B. (1975). *Principles of Psychotherapy*. New York: John Wiley.

Whittaker, A. and McIntosh, B. (2000). 'Changing days'. *British Journal of Learning Disabilities, 28*, 3–8.

Wolfensberger, W. (1972) *The Principle of Normalisation in Human Services*. Toronto: National Institute of Mental Retardation.

Wolfensberger, W. (1983). 'Social role valorisation: a proposed new term for the principle of normalisation'. *Mental Retardation, 21*, 234–9.

Wortman, C.B. and Silver, R.C. (1992). 'Reconsidering assumptions about coping with loss: an overview of current research', in L. Montada, S.H. Filipp and M.J. Lerner (eds), *Life Crises and Experiences of Loss in Adulthood* (pp. 341–65). Hillsdale, NJ: Lawrence Erlbaum Associates.

Wyngaarden, M. (1981). 'Interviewing mentally retarded persons: issues and strategies', in R.H. Bruininks, C.E. Meyers, E.B. Sigford and K.C. Lakin (eds), *Deinstitutionalisation and Community Adjustment of Mentally Retarded People*, Monograph 4. Washington DC: American Association on Mental Deficiency.

Yanok, J. and Beifus, J.A. (1993). 'Communicating about loss and mourning: death education for individuals with mental retardation'. *Mental Retardation, 31*, 144–7.

Zaharia, E.S. and Baumeister, A.A. (1978). 'Technician turnover and absenteeism in public residential facilities'. *American Journal of Mental Deficiency, 82*, 580–93.

Zinkin, L. (1994). 'All's well that ends well. Or is it?' *Group Analysis, 27*, 15–24.

Index

abandonment, feelings of 116
adults with learning disabilities
  behavioural approaches to 5, 7
  bereavement 30–1, 158–9
  emotional lives of 5–8
  friendship needs 22–4, 31
  grief reactions 31–4, 149–50,
    158–9
  labels 14–15
  need for affection 56–7
  and psychotherapy 6, 8–11
  sense of self 57
  social integration 3–5, 13, 23
    see also care in the community
  terminology 14–15
  see also clients; residential homes
aggressive behaviour 27, 31, 32
Allen, P. 18, 19–20
anger 32, 116, 123, 150, 151
apathy 152
art therapy 166
Arthur, A.R. 5
Atkinson, D. 24–5
attachment theory 25–8, 29
attachment(s)
  anxious 25–6
  clients' 148–9, 203
  and empathy 28
  secure and insecure 25, 27, 29
  staff to clients 128–35, 146
  see also keyworkers, emotional
    involvement
attention-seeking 27
autism 140

Barnett, L. 28
Barrett, H. 163
'behavioural management' 7
behavioural problems 6, 66, 137,
  202–3
  aggression 27, 31–2
  manifestation of feelings 7–8, 35,
    125, 134, 154–5, 166

bereavement 30–1, 158–9
Berkson, G. 4
Bicknell, J. 6
Bowlby, J. 25–6, 29
Brechin, A. 174
Brown, H. 12
Burgess, R.G. 46

care in the community 3–5
  and community resources 13
  constraints on clients 23–4
  isolation 4–5, 22, 57
  lack of privacy 22–3
care staff
  devalued role of 12, 63, 102–3,
    142
  feelings of loss 36–7, 128, 178
  guilt 10, 103, 128, 130, 133, 165,
    168
  idealised 54
  job satisfaction 17–18
  letting go 36–7
  need to keep in touch 99–100,
    127, 208, 214
  personal history 28
  role ambiguity 18
  role of 19–22, 25, 146, 155,
    185–6
  and stress 12, 19
  team discussions 173, 177
  training 44–5, 177
  see also keyworkers; staff-client
    relationship
cerebral palsy 41
Chappell, A.L. 22–3
children, in residential care 29–30
children with learning disabilities 27
'circle of support' 175
Clegg, J.A. 18, 20, 21, 26, 27–8,
  68, 117–18
clients
  absence of anger 123, 150
  acting like parent 71–2

attachments 148–9, 203
choice 3, 4, 23
cognitive abilities 157, 163
empowerment 159–60, 174
expanding social networks 13,
    22–3, 58, 172, 174–6
expressing feelings 111–13, 119,
    122–4, 166, 176
fantasy of control 116–17
financial constraints 23
friendships between 4–5, 12–13,
    22–4, 59, 174–6
listening to 13
making sense of communications
    68–9, 146–7
and new keyworker 183–4
numbed feelings 41, 151, 159,
    165, 199, 213
opportunities for going out 23
personal histories 178, 179
physical care 19, 52, 53–4, 64–6
recognising feelings of 31–5,
    133–41, 154, 158–9, 164–7
repeated experiences of separa-
    tion 7, 30, 118, 141, 151–2,
    165, 177
see also staff turnover
respect for 11–12
sense of helplessness 81, 84–5,
    88, 105, 114–18, 151–2, 163–4
social integration 3, 4, 23
symptoms misunderstood 31–2
understanding reasons for separa-
    tion 119–23, 150, 163
see also adults with learning
    disabilities; residential homes
'clinginess' 27
'companion' relationship 20, 21, 54,
    57–60, 70–1, 192
'constant comparison' 48
counter-transference 153, 178
Cue, K.L. 28

Dalal, C. 170
de-institutionalisation
    problems of 3–5
    see also care in the community;
        normalisation; social integration
defence mechanisms, socially struc-
    tured 155–6
Degree of Dependency Rating Scale
    41
denial 135–41, 154–5, 157

dependency 13, 37, 54–5, 119, 153,
    154
    and need for constancy 61, 94,
        147–8
    over-dependence 5, 12, 25,
        172–3, 203–4
    promoting independence 117,
        148, 173, 174
    reinforced 57
    in small residences 22
    see also nurturer role; provider
        role
disabled child, attitude of parents 6,
    26–7
distress
    difficulties expressing 33, 34, 35,
        134, 149–50
    see also grief
Down's syndrome 41
Dozier, M. 28
drama therapy 166

Emerson, P. 18, 31
emotions, help with expressing
    68–9, 119
empathy 28, 138, 165–6

faecal smearing 66
false promises 98, 170
family, contact with 175, 208–9
family therapy 170
feelings
    clients' feelings after separation
        108–24, 183–4
    disguised 123–4, 150–1
    expressing 111–13, 119, 122–4,
        166, 176
    manifested through behaviour
        7–8, 35, 125, 134, 154–5, 166
    numbed 141, 151, 159, 165, 199,
        213
    physical manifestations of
        112–13, 138, 149, 195–6
    recognising 31–5, 133–41, 154,
        158–9, 164–7
    sexual 59, 60
    of staff 36–7, 125–44, 152–8,
        167–8, 178, 187
Firth, H. 24, 175
Flynn, M.C. 43
Fredman, G. 170
friendships, between clients 4–5,
    12–13, 22–4, 59, 174–6

Gallimore, R. 27
Ghazziudin, M. 32
gifts 81–2
grief 109–14
  expressing through verbal
    communication 149
  and medication 33
  see also bereavement
grief reactions 31–4, 149–50, 158–9
grieving process
  difficulties of 166
  facilitating 35, 158–60, 162
  understanding 178

Harper, D.C. 18, 32–3, 149
head banging 35
'holding in mind' 61, 75

interviews
  analysis of data 47–9
  qualitative 51
  of residents 43, 181–4, 188–201
  semi-structured 42, 45, 46
  of staff 185–7
  tape-recording 43, 45
  types of questions 43, 46–7

Jones, D 163

Kauffman, J. 151, 177–8
keeping in touch 83–5, 97–102,
    170, 214
  discouraged by employers 100–1
  postcards 84, 110, 197, 201
keyworkers
  client's perception of 147
  clients' protective feelings
    towards 72, 125
  companion role 20, 21, 54,
    57–60, 70–1, 192
  constancy 60–1, 147
  denial 135–41, 154–5, 157
  dispensability 62–3, 130, 140,
    141, 143, 155
  emotional involvement 73–6,
    128–35, 138, 146, 171–2, 215
    and distance 74, 105, 172
    emotional overload 25, 148,
      167, 172, 173
    over-involvement 74, 97
    and uncomfortable feelings 67
  as 'enablers' 174, 175–6
  family role 71–4, 147

feelings of inadequacy 62
importance in client's life 2, 21,
    135–9, 141–4, 155, 164–5
indispensability 133, 153–4, 155
and intimacy 58–9, 62, 74–6, 77,
    147, 167
and jealousy of new care staff
    127, 143, 211
'meaning maker' role 20–1, 68–9,
    76
'mutual' relationship 20, 21
'nurturer' role 56–7, 69, 76, 148
organisational responsibilities 64,
    66–8, 172
as parent figure 71–2, 147
'provider' role 53–5, 64–8, 76,
    148
reciprocity/mutuality in relation-
    ship 60, 63, 70–1, 121, 147
recognising own feelings 167–8,
    178
role of 14, 52–77, 171–4
rotation of 79–80, 143–4, 156
self-devaluation 141–4, 155, 156,
    165
sexual feelings towards 59, 60
'shadowing' old keyworkers 169
sharing responsibility 174
taking holidays 132
time to reflect 179
training and qualifications 44–5
underestimating clients' reactions
    1–2, 62–3, 130, 142, 157–8
  see also denial
ways of leaving 78–107
  see also care staff; staff-client rela-
    tionship
kindness 56–7

Landesmann-Dwyer, S. 4
Lansdall-Welfare, R. 18, 26, 27–8
Lanyado, M. 30
learned helplessness 152, 163
loss see bereavement; grief; separa-
    tion

managers, support of staff 144, 156,
    163, 173, 179, 210
'meaning maker' relationship 20–1,
    68–9, 76
medication, for symptoms of grief
    33
Menzies, I.E.P. 155

'mutual' relationship 20, 21
'mutuality of loss' 178

normalisation 3, 6, 22–3
'nurturer' relationship 56–7, 69, 76,
    148

'open coding' 47–8
Oswin, M. 33, 35, 149, 159

parent-child bonding, and learning
    disability 26–7
passivity 32
Perske, R. 117
privacy 176
'provider' relationship 20–1, 53–5,
    64–8, 76, 148
psychodynamics 6, 178
psychotherapy 6, 8–11
    termination of 36, 158, 170

questions, open and closed 43

Rapley, M. 24, 175
reality and fantasy, distinction
    between 157
regression 102, 127, 130–1, 133,
    134, 150
'relationship map' 175
relationships
    early experiences 26
    'internal working models' 26
    see also attachment; staff-client
        relationship
research
    analysis of data 47–9
    conduct of 39–51
    interpretation of data 48–9, 51
    limitations of 49–51
resident study 40–4
    characteristics of residents 41–2,
        49, 50
    consent 42
    interviews 42–4, 50, 51
residential homes
    depersonalisation 156
    'family-like' homes 4–5, 8, 22
    and friendships between residents
        4–5, 12–13, 22–4, 59, 174–6
    promoting independence 117,
        148, 173, 174
    social defence systems 156
    support between residents 117–18

see also care in the community;
    staff turnover; staff-client rela-
    tionship
'response sets' 50
Robson, C. 46
Rosenberg, M.L. 37, 85, 154, 157,
    159

sadness 116, 121, 122–3, 148
Salzberger-Wittenberg, I. 158
saying goodbye
    avoiding 85, 86–7, 89, 105, 157,
        162–3
    difficulties of 157–8
    importance of 158–60
    parties 78, 82–3, 95, 96, 104,
        106
    see also separation
Schaefer, C.E. 29–30
'secondary handicap' 6–7
self-injury 32, 35, 55
separation
    abrupt departures 79–81, 86–91,
        105, 131, 164, 199
    avoiding saying goodbye 85,
        86–7, 89, 105, 157, 162–3
    clean break 98, 100, 170
    clients' acceptance of 118–24,
        150–1, 152
    clients' accounts of 78–85, 182
    clients' feelings after 108–24,
        183–4
    clients' reactions to 92, 93,
        106–7, 108–14, 131–2, 205–6
    difficulties of saying goodbye
        157–8
    'dysfunctional' reactions to 32–3
    goodbye parties 78, 82–3, 95, 96,
        104, 106
    and grief 109–14
    handover to new keyworkers
        90–1, 117, 190, 197–8,
        215–16
        planning for 95, 169–71,
            178–9
    helping clients to adjust to 34–7
    importance of saying goodbye
        158–60
    keeping in touch 83–5, 97–102,
        170, 214
    link with bereavement 109–10,
        111, 113, 125, 149, 158, 210
    opportunity for review 170–1

separation *continued*
  planned endings 91–5, 107, 159,
    163
  and pleasant rituals 81–3, 95–7,
    106
  preparation for 36, 81, 86, 87,
    90–5, 158–60, 205
    recommendations 161–80
    timing 92–4, 96, 163
  process of 78–107
  staff accounts of 85–105, 186
  staff feelings 125–44, 152–8,
    167–8, 187
  staff support and supervision
    102–5, 144, 161–2, 166–8,
    176–9, 210
  talking about 78, 95, 119–20,
    131, 156–7, 162–4
  and transition 95, 170
'shadowing' 169
Siebold, C. 36, 153
Sigelman, C.K. 43
Silver, R.C. 81
Sinason, V. 6–7, 18, 34–5, 123, 151
Smith, H. 12
social integration 3–5, 13, 23
social networks
  expanding 13, 58, 172, 174–6
  importance of 21–2
social skills 24, 175, 176
socially structured defence mecha-
    nisms 155–6
staff study 44–7
  characteristics of residents 45, 49
  characteristics of staff 44–5, 49
  consent 45
  interviews 45–7
staff turnover 3, 17–18, 61, 104,
    177
  effect on clients 127, 213
  and keyworking relationship 21
  see also clients, repeated experi-
    ences of separation

staff-client relationship 5, 11–12,
    19–38
  and attachment theory 25–8
  boundaries 59, 97–8, 120, 150,
    173–4
  client's perception of 21, 181–2
  developing new form of 98–9,
    129
  ending of 2–3, 28–37, 148–52
  false expectations 24–5
  meaning of 19–28, 146–8
  and parent-child relationship
    71–3
  staff perception of 185–6
  and trust 88–9, 117, 159
  types of 20–1
  unequal 172
  see also care staff; keyworkers
Swain, J. 152, 174
Swanson, A.J. 29–30

Terry, P. 154–5
'theoretical memos' 48
time/future, concepts of 157, 163
transference 178
trauma, exacerbating handicap 6–7

visual aids 166

Wadsworth, J.S. 18, 32–3, 149
Weiner, I.B. 36
withdrawal 27, 131–2, 134, 150,
    206–7, 217
  and bereavement 31
Wolfensberger, W. 3
Wortman, C.B. 81
Wyngaarden, M. 43

Zinkin, L. 81, 158

Compiled by Sue Carlton